The World Is

FAT

The World Is

FAT

The Fads, Trends, Policies, and Products
That Are Fattening the Human Race

BARRY POPKIN

AVERY

a member of Penguin Group (USA) Inc.

New York

Published by the Penguin Group

Penguin Group (USA) Inc., 375 Hudson Street, New York, New York 10014, USA • Penguin Group
(Canada), 90 Eglinton Avenue East, Suite 700, Toronto, Ontario M4P 2Y3, Canada (a division of
Pearson Canada Inc.) • Penguin Books Ltd, 80 Strand, London WC2R 0RL, England • Penguin Ireland,
25 St Stephen's Green, Dublin 2, Ireland (a division of Penguin Books Ltd) • Penguin Group (Australia),
250 Camberwell Road, Camberwell, Victoria 3124, Australia (a division of Pearson Australia
Group Pty Ltd) • Penguin Books India Pvt Ltd, 11 Community Centre, Panchsheel Park,
New Delhi–110 017, India • Penguin Group (NZ), 67 Apollo Drive, Rosedale, North Shore 0632,
New Zealand (a division of Pearson New Zealand Ltd) • Penguin Books (South Africa) (Pty) Ltd,
24 Sturdee Avenue, Rosebank, Johannesburg 2196, South Africa

Penguin Books Ltd, Registered Offices:
80 Strand, London WC2R 0RL, England

Most Avery books are available at special quantity discounts for bulk purchase for sales promotions, premiums, fund-
raising, and educational needs. Special books or book excerpts also can be created to fit specific needs. For details,
write Penguin Group (USA) Inc. Special Markets, 375 Hudson Street, New York, NY 10014.

Library of Congress Cataloging-in-Publication Data
Popkin, Barry M.
The world is fat : the fads, trends, policies, and products that are fattening the human race / Barry Popkin.
p.   cm.
Includes bibliographical references and index.
ISBN 978-1-58333-313-6
1. Obesity.   2. Obesity—Social aspects.   3. Body, Human—Social aspects.   I. Title.
RC552.O25P67   2008   2008039158
362.196'398—dc22

Printed in the United States of America
1   3   5   7   9   10   8   6   4   2

BOOK DESIGN BY MEIGHAN CAVANAUGH

While the author has made every effort to provide accurate telephone numbers and Internet addresses
at the time of publication, neither the publisher nor the author assumes any responsibility for errors,
or for changes that occur after publication. Further, the publisher does not have any control over
and does not assume any responsibility for author or third-party websites or their content.

For Matt, Anne-Linda,
and my family

CONTENTS

The World Is
FAT

INTRODUCTION

I first became interested in nutrition in 1965, when I spent a year in India as part of a fully funded college year abroad. I lived in Old Delhi in a *jhuggi-jhopri* cluster—the Indian term for the shantytowns that are built wherever land is available. It was one of the most densely populated areas in the world, a residential slum teeming with life. People lived on top of one another in primitive one-story structures in a vibrant cacophony of smells, noises, and dress. Sanitation was horrendous and poverty was the norm. Hunger was widespread.

After returning to the United States and completing college, I got a job at the U.S. Office of Economic Opportunity. I was also actively involved with the McGovern Committee on Hunger in America, which was creating and expanding a range of programs intended to reduce undernutrition. Thus began my career studying food and nutrition from the perspective of economics. In the 1960s and 1970s, poverty and hunger were the big problems—both in the United States and abroad. In the 1980s, obesity began to replace hunger as the main nutritional problem in the United States and Europe, but hunger was still the big problem across the developing world. Today, however, obesity is a problem of epidemic proportions around the globe. This book is about the changes that have caused this seismic shift—big-picture trends in technology, globalization, government policy, and the food industry that interact with individual choices about how we eat and how we live.

I've lived and worked around the world, studying how lifestyle changes over the long term have affected the body composition of Americans, Chinese, Russians, Brazilians, Filipinos, and many others. I'm one of the few experts—if not the only expert—to have conducted large-scale, longitudinal surveys following obesity on a global scale. I've been studying more than thirty-five years of data on the dietary trends of more than eighty thousand Americans. I'm involved in the obesity and physical activity component of the National Longitudinal Survey of Adolescent Health, which has been following twenty thousand teen-agers since 1995. (A further survey is being done on the former teens who now are entering the twenty-six- to thirty-two-year-old age group.)

Similarly, I've been following more than twenty-two thousand Chinese from more than two hundred communities for twenty years, more than eleven thousand Russians from more than three hundred communities for fifteen years, and many others for decades. In rapidly changing China, we're taking intense snapshots every two to three years of the diets, activity patterns, weight, and height of the participants in one of our studies. We're also studying how their communities, jobs, and incomes are changing.

To help reveal how our nutritional lives have changed since World War II for those of us in the West and how they've changed since the 1980s in the developing world, throughout the book I'll be referring to four families from my long-term research as well as my own family life from the 1950s. (To protect the privacy of the participants in my research, these families are representative composites of actual fami-lies I have studied.) We'll see how the Jones and Garcia families in the present-day United States eat, drink, and move. And we'll see how the dietary and physical activity patterns of the Desais, a family from 1980s India, contrast with those of the Patels, a present-day Indian family. It's also important to put the changes of the past decades into context. In the first chapter, I'll take a brief look at the major shifts in the human diet from the Paleolithic period to the present, and how those dietary changes were accompanied by changes in body composition.

I'll address some big questions: Are today's beverages—the ones that contain tons of added sugars—the cause of this crisis? What role does fast food play in weight gain and obesity? What about the Wal-Mart-ization of the globe? Is the availability of processed foods just about everywhere making us fat and unhealthy? Can the obesity epidemic be explained simply as a loss of social norms and controls in an era of gluttony and sloth? Or is not food but our lack of movement the culprit, as the food industry has claimed? What role do parents and schools play? Why are so many poor people overweight?

On the most basic level, however, this is the story of how progress often comes with a cost. It's an understatement to say that our lives have greatly improved from preagricultural times to the present. But there have been trade-offs. For example, the development of agriculture allowed the world's first great civilizations to arise. As we'll see, however, this resulted in the varied diet of hunter-gatherers giving way to a diet based on only a few crops, and an increase in famine and disease. More recently, technology has significantly—and rapidly— changed our lives, both at work and at home, and globalization has increased our access to ideas, people, and products from all corners of the world. Progress, without a doubt. But not without the major cost—in both health and economic terms—of global obesity.

I grew up in the 1950s in Superior, Wisconsin, a small town of population thirty-five thousand similar to thousands of towns of that era. My parents, brother, sister, and I were tied into a network of neighbors and relatives who acted as a large extended family—we lived next to my grandmother for the first nine years of my life, and living next to her were an uncle and aunt. We were a typical multi-generational American family. Our neighbors were either friends of the family, members of our synagogue, or parents of my classmates. Ours was very much an open neighborhood where I could go into any house at any time and be welcomed. Few of the mothers worked, and most all the dads worked close to home.

My friends and I played the sports of the season on an empty corner lot—football, baseball, and ice-skating. In the cold winter the city would flood the football field and, voila, we had an ice-skating rink. I walked or biked everywhere. I lived a half-mile from elementary school and two miles from high school. On Saturday mornings, my friends and I would walk three miles to the local cinema to catch a double feature. The only time I used a bus was to go to the dental office of my cousin Sherman in Duluth—about seven miles away. I was often driven to and from religious school, which was about three miles away. My father would go to work on Sundays for a few hours at the furniture store he owned, drop us on the way, and pick us up after that.

Daily gym classes at school included calisthenics such as jumping jacks, push-ups, and other strenuous exercises. We were always very physically active. Everyone in class broke a sweat, and we usually had to take showers at the end of class.

During the summer I mowed lawns, worked in other people's gardens, and babysat until I was about fifteen years old, when I managed a Babe Ruth baseball league, and I had newspaper routes at various times. In the winter, I shoveled snow—tons of it. Superior has some of the coldest weather and largest snowfalls in the United States. While I may have worked more than many of my friends, none of these activities was outside the norm. We were active, and we weren't overweight.

My family wasn't wealthy, but we enjoyed a decent standard of living in that Kodachrome world that was 1950s America.

Our meals were quite basic. Breakfast was a ready-to-eat cereal. I liked my cereals on the soggy side, so I usually ate Wheaties or cornflakes. My brother and sister didn't like soggy cereal, so we had to fight to get my mother to keep two cereals—Wheat Chex for them and Wheaties or cornflakes for me. On special weekend occasions we might have pancakes or waffles with a glass of milk. Lunch consisted of a sandwich, macaroni and cheese, soup, or pasta. When I was in junior high school I fell in love with Franco-American canned spaghetti and, because it was inexpensive, we ate it once or twice a week. We drank milk for lunch but often had water with dinner, and the evening meal was frequently chicken or pot roast alongside potatoes, or spaghetti with homemade sauce. Mashed potatoes and corn were two of the few vegetables I ate. I remember vividly that my father would not eat vegetables at all, except for his beloved pickles.

Preserving and preparing certain foods were big family events. Every summer we bought bushels of cucumbers and created a family assembly line to clean and pickle them. We all pitched in the few times each year we made French-fried onion rings. I learned a lot about baking from helping my grandmother make pies. I also learned how to poach eggs and do other basic cooking tasks.

Shopping was a major family event. My mother and our neighbors assiduously clipped coupons and planned their weekly grocery shopping to coincide with sales at the two or three larger grocery stores. All of them by today's standards were fairly small with narrow aisles, and offered several types of cereal, maybe only one variety of coffee, flour, and other basics, and, notably, just a few types of soft drinks, such as Coca-Cola, orange pop, and 7-Up. The dairy aisle had butter—margarine had not yet been widely distributed and was unavailable in Wisconsin (in fact, it was illegal there until 1967)—and whole milk.

In the winter, my mother often bought frozen vegetables. We purchased potatoes in huge bags during the late summer or early fall when they were very cheap and kept them in our cold cellar—a true unfinished basement—where we also kept the pickles and other food my mother canned, including tomatoes and green beans. During my younger years, my mother and the other women in our town went to a community cannery in the summer and fall to can their fruits and vegetables.

We never brought cooked food into the house for a meal. The only exceptions were my mother's potluck suppers, sewing circle, and card clubs, when each woman would bring a special pastry she had made that morning. This might be mandelbrot, poppy-seed Bundt cake, kamish bread, or meat blintzes—ethnic pastries linked to the women's Eastern European backgrounds that they perfected over their adulthood.

It was the same at my friends' homes, although the pastry recipes were more likely to have come from Scandinavia or Belgium. Sometimes, parents would bring in prepared dishes for a potluck meal at our school, but nobody purchased prepared food in those days, not even cakes. I hadn't even heard of a store-prepared cake until I attended my first wedding.

A few times each summer, my dad would take us for a drive along the Lake Superior shoreline at sunset. We would stop at the local A&W Root Beer stand and a carhop would come out to serve us. Or we might go to the Dairy Queen. Only once or twice a year did we go out to eat a meal, usually at Eddie's Steak House, which was just outside of town. It was a fairly plain local joint by current standards, but to us then it was a fancy place. These were special occasions—times when we got to drink soft drinks—a rare treat.

Introduction

————

When I last studied the Jones family, in 2006, Ellen Jones was a schoolteacher and Bob Jones worked at an insurance agency. Their son, Scott, was nine and their daughter, Linda, was fifteen. Both children led lives unheard of by those of us who grew up in the 1950s. They lived in a suburb outside Cleveland.

Scott and Linda never walk to school. Scott is driven by either Ellen or Bob and Linda is picked up by a school bus at the corner of their block. Ellen prepares a big chart each week that shows Scott's and Linda's schedules and who will drive them where. Bob's and Ellen's lives are organized completely around these transportation responsibilities, including taking Linda to her dance and music lessons and taking Scott to his soccer practices and games or to play at a friend's if the friend lives more than a block away. Both children have fancy bikes, but rarely use them.

Linda babysat for several years until she reached an age when going out with her friends was more important. Scott hasn't worked yet, but he is paid a small sum by his parents to do some chores around the house. Times have changed—when I grew up we were expected to do chores as part of just normal daily living. Bob and Ellen, on the other hand, almost have to beg Scott to carry out the garbage bags to the trash can.

Linda was enrolled in music and dance lessons for a time, and Scott added lacrosse to his soccer playing. As they got older, however, both of them wandered away from sports. Scott did a little skateboarding, but eventually stopped that also.

The family spends a lot of time together on weekday nights and on Sundays watching television. Sundays are reserved for the Cleveland Browns in the winter and Cleveland Indians in the summer. The evening meal is eaten on TV trays, and all four Joneses stay glued to the TV until bedtime. At first, the family owned only one set and watched their programs together. Eventually, the children got their own TVs. The family used to share a computer, too, but now that Linda used it to write papers for school, her parents were considering buying a second computer.

In school, Scott's and Linda's gym classes didn't include any exercises or sports but mainly were about sex education and health education. They never broke a sweat in PE class.

Everyone in the family eats some breakfast. For Linda, this usually consists of a Pop-Tart or two on the run as she races to get the school bus. Scott favors the sugar-sweetened cereals such as Kellogg's Frosted Flakes and General Mills' Chocolate Lucky Charms. On weekends, he loves to eat waffles and often talks his father into taking him to the International House of Pancakes.

Both Linda and Scott buy lunch at school. Linda is old enough to be allowed to eat off campus once a week—she usually chooses McDonald's. The school cafeteria has several fast-food companies bring in the food for lunches; she likes the Pizza Hut foods best. Scott's school has a cafeteria where meals are prepared. His most frequent meal is French fries and cheeseburgers. Recently, the school has begun to serve more vegetables and even salads, but they still serve fried foods, including fries and, often, fried chicken. Scott always buys a twelve-ounce bottle of juice when he forgets to bring a beverage from home, while Linda is able to buy soft drinks at her high school. Ellen, being a teacher, often eats the same cafeteria meals as her children unless she is on one of her repeated attempts to diet, when she might bring a salad to work. Bob eats lunch with his colleagues—usually at Burger King or KFC.

Dinners are usually take-out affairs. Most nights during the week, Bob and Ellen buy prepared food dishes like roasted chicken and mashed potatoes at the local supermarket, pizza, or Chinese take-out.

About once a week, Ellen buys semiprepared food such as spaghetti or ravioli and heats it at home. In any case, the microwave is used far more often than the cooktop or oven.

Perhaps not surprisingly, each member of the family has a weight problem. Bob slowly developed a serious weight problem, and has hypertension. He is five-feet-ten and weighs over two hundred pounds. His doctor said he is prediabetic. Since he is only forty-one years old, he isn't worried. Ellen is a little plump—she's five-feet-five and weighs 155 pounds. She never exercises, and when she periodically tries to cut calories at lunch and dinner by eating salads, she always adds a generous portion of ranch dressing on top. Linda was pudgy at age five, and by age ten, when she first menstruated, she was slightly fat. She has gotten somewhat fatter over the past five years and is constantly upset about her weight. Linda is just an inch taller than her mother but weighs thirteen pounds more, so while she is not obese by any standards, she is quite a bit chunkier than the television actresses whose shows she likes to watch. Scott is also pudgy. He weighs 135 pounds, but he's just nearing five feet in height. There is a strong possibility that he'll have a growth spurt and thin out. Otherwise, he'll be overweight when he reaches Linda's age.

Cesar and Ana Garcia immigrated to the United States from small villages in the Chiapas region of Mexico in 1985. They met in the United States and married in 1990 when they were twenty-five years old. They have four children, ranging from five to fifteen years old.

In the communities where Cesar and Ana grew up, there were no roads or electricity until 2000. They attended elementary school, but only Cesar went beyond. He did not finish high school, however. Both worked first as migrant laborers picking fruit and vegetables in California and Arizona; then Cesar got a job in construction, and with his intelligence and hard work he quickly became a skilled carpenter. He learned to speak English and is now foreman for one of the crews of a large construction company. Ana works cleaning homes and has learned some English, although she is not fluent.

The Garcias live in a Los Angeles suburb in a nice, small, three-bedroom house. The children ride buses to school, which is over ten miles away for Daniel, the eldest child, while the elementary school is only two miles from home. The youngest of the children, Felix, is taken to a friend's house where he is cared for during the day; he'll be eligible for kindergarten next year. Maria is older and takes care of herself, and she sometimes helps with the other kids.

For a few years, Daniel played soccer with kids in the street but he no longer participates. Instead, he watches television with his siblings, at least four hours daily. Felix is particularly fascinated by TV and watches it almost all day while he is in day care. I'd guess that Felix watches TV at least ten hours a day.

The younger daughter, Rosario, attends an after-school program with her friends and rides a bus home. This program is rather loosely organized and passive; the kids get snacks and are allowed to just talk or play games, but there are no organized activities of any sort. Thus the children just sit or stand in a group and talk. They are never physically active. The older siblings like to hang out after school with their friends.

The meals that the Garcias eat in the United States are very different from the meals they ate in Mexico. When Ana and Cesar first came to the United States, they ate rice, beans, and tortillas. But with added income and more shopping opportunities, their diet has changed and the children constantly push their parents to let them eat the foods they see on TV. When Ana was growing up in Mexico, her mother prepared her tortillas at home, and they were very healthful, as she soaked the corn in lime juice and water, ground it herself, and baked the tortillas over a small wood fire. There were just a few neighborhood *tiendas* at which to shop, but once Ana moved to the United States, she found the *tiendas* sold beer and soft drinks (*refrescos*) and also sugared juice drinks (*aguas frescas*) along with lots of snack food. After Ana and Cesar married and moved to Los Angeles, they had many neighborhood *tiendas* to choose from, but they also found that at Wal-Mart they could buy very cheaply the same *refrescos* the *tiendas* sold, and even tortillas and inexpensive meat. The biggest dietary change they made was from drinking water in Mexico to drinking sweetened drinks and beer here.

For breakfast, the family eats fried beef tacos with cheese and sour cream. The children often have soft drinks for breakfast, although little Felix loves fruit punch or fruit juice to which they add extra sugar. The other children like Coca-Cola for breakfast. The parents drink coffee with cream and lots of sugar.

For lunch, the children eat what is provided at either school or day care. The schools provide them with whole milk and juice and for all three, pizza and a soft drink is their normal lunch. Felix eats enchiladas and fruit drinks for lunch, and his snacks are usually some type of cake or cookies and soft drinks.

Dinner is always prepared by Ana. She buys tortillas at the grocery store and serves them hot with butter. She also often makes chicken or pork soup with spices such as achiote seeds, which she finishes with a little sprinkled cheese on top. Soft drinks are consumed by all, unless Cesar decides to have a beer.

All the Garcias are heavy. And their problems are just getting started, as we'll see.

Rahul Desai and his wife, Manju, were living in the state of Uttar Pradesh when I met them in the 1980s. They had a small plot of land and owned one cow and one water buffalo. Both the cow and water buffalo provided milk for the family, from which they made yogurt and ghee, a clarified butter that lasts a long time when stored without exposure to the air.

Both Rahul and Manju worked all day in the fields. In addition to providing milk, the water buffalo helped them plow the land. Many of their neighbors, however, did everything by hand. All families in the village planted wheat and chickpeas. In the 1960s they grew sugarcane, but a decline in world prices during the 1970s made it unprofitable and they shifted to these other crops. (Sugar prices move up and down as Brazil, Cuba, China, European countries, the United States, and other major sugar producers have good and bad years and as political support for price subsidies rise and fall in various countries.) While the plowing and tilling at the beginning of the season was done with the help of the water buffalo, the threshing and the cleaning of the grain was done by hand. To get their crops to market, the grains and chickpeas were carried on the water buffalo's back while Rahul and Manju walked alongside. Their work throughout the year was extremely labor-intensive.

At home, the work continued. The Desais built and rebuilt their house, which was made of mud. Manju used no commercially prepared foods. Their basic meals were chapatis—breads made from unleavened dough—yogurt, and some cooked lentils. Ghee was a major component of all meals. The lentils were cooked in it and chapatis were spread with it. Only the yogurt—made from very rich water buffalo milk—didn't have ghee added to it. The fat content of ghee is among the highest in the world, as I can attest from eating ice cream, milk, and yogurt made with it. With a fat content of about 10 percent (this is two and a half times the fat content of cow's milk in the United States), it makes the water buffalo milk and yogurt rich and tasty.

Their four children—two boys and two girls—were ages three,

six, eight, and ten years old. The two boys, Amit and Ajay, briefly attended elementary school before leaving to work with the family. The school costs for the year—for books, clothing, minor gifts, and other expenses—were beyond what the family could afford with so many mouths to feed. The younger girls—Aishani and Achla—played around the house and learned to do chores as they were able. It was likely that neither girl would ever attend school.

All of the family members were very thin; the mother looked the thinnest. She was only four-feet-eight and weighed seventy-five pounds. The father was five feet tall and weighed one hundred pounds. The children suffered from diarrhea when they were young, and they were shorter for their age than normal (i.e., stunted). Amit and Ajay were about 50 inches and 46 inches tall, respectively, while the girls were 33 inches and only 34 inches, each weighing just twenty-four pounds. To me, they all seemed very undernourished.

None of the Desais had ever visited a big city. Lucknow (population 2.5 million), capital of Uttar Pradesh, is more than two hundred kilometers away and beyond their comprehension. The local market town, Mahrajganj (pop. 6,000), is located about forty kilometers from the larger city of Rae Bareli. Only Lucknow and Rae Bareli are big enough to be on any maps. The Desais transported grain and chick-peas to buyers in Mahrajganj, which is just fifteen kilometers away. Wealthier farmers take their wheat to a mill that's run with an electric generator, but the Desais can't afford this; they sell their products to small buyers for a small profit. These middlemen handle all the processing and then transport the grain to larger buyers who pay more in Rae Bareli.

I returned in 2006 to visit the Patels, a family of five, who also live in Uttar Pradesh. Gopal and Noopur and their three children,

Rimi, Manish, and Mona, have a small plot of land similar to that of the Desais. However, they have electricity, a tiny motorized plow, and they jointly own a tractor with several neighbors. They grow fruits and vegetables and raise egg-laying hens. They often go to the nearby city of Rae Bareli to sell their produce and eggs to a middleman, who in turn takes these products to even larger cities such as Lucknow and the industrial town of Kanpur, with its population of over four million.

The Patels work hard, but do not expend half as much physical energy as did the Desais. They have one hired worker who comes from a nearby village. He sleeps in the fields during the planting and harvesting seasons and is paid just thirty to forty rupees, or less than a dollar a day, for ten to twelve hours of very hard work, plus a simple meal of rice and lentils that he is given in the middle of the day.

Noopur no longer makes her own ghee, but rather buys huge cans of vanaspati, a fully or partially hydrogenated vegetable cooking oil that is usually made from palm oil. She buys her chapatis from Mahrajganj, the small market town, unless they have a big outing and go to Rae Bareli, where they buy large sacks of flour to make chapatis. She also buys yogurt, though the family does keep a small cow to provide milk for them all.

The Patels' house is made of bricks and has electricity. They own two radios and recently bought a new black-and-white TV, which is linked to a tiny direct satellite in their village and linked from there to a large satellite in Lucknow. The state government subsidizes this TV system. Whenever possible, the family sits around the TV to learn about the world outside their village. There are programs on politics, agriculture, literacy, ways to prepare food so it does not spoil, and a daily UNICEF-funded program about ways to prevent diarrhea. There are no sitcoms, dramas, or other types of programming along the lines of what we see in the United States.

The family eats all their meals together. Breakfast consists of yogurt, chapati, and dhal (dhal, or dal, is a bean harvested solely for the dry grain by stripping off its outer hulls and splitting the core bean). They share fried eggs four times a week, and lots of vanaspati is used with the chapatis. Lunch is similar. They have chicken or pork for dinner four to five times a week, which come from live chickens and tiny pieces of pork they purchase at the market in Mahrajganj or from a neighbor who sells them. Obviously, they are not vegetarians.

The children are pushed by their parents to study very hard. Next year, if their oldest son passes certain exams, they will send him to a boarding school in Lucknow. They hope he will continue to do well so he can go on to college.

The greatest difference between the Desais and Patels is their body composition. Noopur has a belly that protrudes from her sari. Gopal has a large belly and is very proud of it. Gopal has been feeling somewhat tired and thirsty all the time without knowing why. His two sons and daughter are all taller than their parents were at the same age. The older son is, at twelve years of age, on his way to developing his own large belly.

How we have come to live in a world in which families as diverse as the Patels, the Garcias, and the Joneses have strikingly similar problems with obesity and illness is what I intend to explain in this book. I will show how the global economy has shaped our health, well-being, and everyday lives. I will show that our biology, which was shaped by millions of years of evolution, is not prepared for our modern society, which has profoundly changed how we eat, drink, and move.

1

A Brief History of
the Modern Diet

Today, over 1.6 billion people in the world are overweight and obese, well over 230 million have diabetes, and more than 1.5 billion have hypertension. In the 1950s, there were less than 100 million overweight and obese individuals, and one-twentieth that number with diabetes and hypertension. Over the last half-century, we've experienced rapid and widespread changes in how we eat, drink, and move. We live in a fat world because the human body—a product of many millennia of evolution—can't keep up with these changes. How we react to the different components of our diet—both beverages and foods—and to the movement patterns of our daily lives goes back millions of years.

We don't have a lot of facts about the human diet and lifestyle before the Upper Paleolithic period, which began about forty thousand years ago and is characterized by the emergence of stone tools. In many ways, man ate and drank in the healthiest manner possible during the Upper Paleolithic period, when humans were nomadic hunter-gatherers. The use or control of fire has been documented during this period in many locations. About 50 to 80 percent of food came from plants and 20 to 50 percent from animals. Coastal dwellers received more nutrition from fishing and inland residents received more from hunting, which progressed over time from small to large game. With this varied diet—which was far more diverse than diets consumed today—scholars think Paleolithic humans were taller than later man, with more robust skeletons and musculature. Paleolithic men and women had short life spans but reasonable nutritional status—infectious diseases were the major cause of morbidity and death.

The basic diet—which varied across the seasons—came from the seeds of grasses, tree nuts, roots and tubers, fish, and aquatic mammals. People living at this time consumed no grains, and no dairy products other than breast milk. They drank water. The meat of land animals had a lower fat content, an even lower proportion of saturated fat, and five times the proportion of polyunsaturated fat than the domestic animal meat consumed today. Fiber intake was very high, some from indigestible roughage. Among those who survived infectious disease and lived to be older, chronic diseases such as diabetes, obesity, heart disease, cancer, dental caries, and bone problems such as osteoporosis were unknown.

Around 10,000 to 11,000 BCE, the development of agriculture changed everything. The varied diet of the Paleolithic gave way to a diet based on a few cereal crops—or even just one crop. The introduction of farming created food surpluses, which allowed the great civilizations of Mesopotamia, the Indus Valley, China, and the Americas to develop. Barley was the chief crop in Mesopotamia; wheat and barley in the Indus valley; corn throughout the Americas for the Aztecs, Mayan, and Incas; and rice, wheat, and millet in China. Recent discoveries show that the Andean cultivation of squash began around this time as well. Agriculture became dominant at different times in different regions—by about 7000 BCE in Southeast Asia and by 500 BCE in Mexico. Famine and disease increased. Hunting became much less important, and in some societies in Europe and Asia it turned into an elite-only pastime. People got shorter—height declined on average by about four inches from about 11,000 BCE to the time of Christ. Farming was a mixed blessing, but with its surpluses and its harnessing of animal power to help people avoid manual labor it paved the way for the modern world.

While sheep and later cows and goats were domesticated beginning twelve thousand to thirteen thousand years ago, there is no evidence that they were used for dairy products until much later. Speculation dates the earliest consumption of milk to 9000 BCE, but it might have begun as late as 4000 BCE. There is little evidence that livestock was a major source of nutrition—except in limited sub-populations in Mongolia and Central Asia—until about a thousand years ago. Generally, the proportion of meat we consumed significantly declined, while vegetable foods surged to as much as 90 percent of the human diet. As time passed, fewer people were involved in farming as specialization increased in metalworking, woodworking, and other early skilled crafts.

Famine began to decline in the last three hundred to four hundred years when we entered the modern era, which was dominated initially by trade in sugar and spices, in terms of the income it brought the nations of Europe. Only in the last two hundred years have manufactured goods such as textiles, tools, and processed foods become a part of global trade. (Food trade is mostly a post–World War II phenomenon—not until then did agricultural technology substantially increase productivity and the production of wheat, soybeans, corn, and rice.) New technologies and ideas, such as natural fertilizers and crop rotation systems, began to be applied to agriculture three hundred to four hundred years ago. But only in the last sixty years have we seen large advances in irrigation, transportation within and across national and regional borders, and changes in seed technology, fertilizer use, and chemicals to control insects. All of these advances helped reduce the impact of climatic fluctuations on the availability of food.

Much of what we eat today emerged during the modern era—a period of global trade and exploration. Many foods that we identify with ethnic cuisines were introduced to their respective countries after the Americas and the Caribbean region were discovered. The tomato was introduced to Italy in the mid-1550s from South America. The chili pepper—found by Columbus in the Caribbean and introduced to Spain in 1494—was ultimately introduced to India, Thailand, and the Szechwan region of China from North America. The potato and chocolate were also introduced to Europe from South America. In the United States, what would the South be like without molasses and yams, which originated in the Caribbean and China? (Many argue there is strong evidence that the sweet potato or yam comes from the Americas.) What about Australia and New Zealand, without sheep, which came from either Central Asia, Iraq, or East Asia? It is difficult to overstate the impact of trade on our world over the past half-millennium.

During the Industrial Revolution, the animal protein content of our diet began to increase. Diets became more diversified as the foods of the Americas and other areas of the globe conquered by the European powers were integrated into the Western diet. The stature of adults in Europe and the United States increased two to four inches on average. The consumption of starchy foods such as bread and potatoes decreased and the consumption of sugar, vegetables, and fruits increased. The greater amounts of animal protein and fat, as well as changes in our knowledge of foods, helped reduce scurvy and undernutrition. The introduction of techniques for milling grain led to a decline in fiber intake, removed the B vitamins in grains that are located near the outer husk, and resulted in a short-term increase in deficiency diseases like pellagra and beriberi, which were caused by the excessive milling of corn and rice, respectively. In fact, pellagra was the great scourge of the American South as late as the early 1900s. Only when an epidemiologist, Joseph Goldberger, showed that pellagra was linked to diet and that baker's yeast could prevent it did we begin to learn more about it.

The Industrial Revolution was also characterized by increases in social inequality, the clustering of the poor in slums and ghettoes, and the evolution of new dietary problems related to the early weaning of infants. Breast-feeding declined when women went to work in factories and child labor became important. At the same time, poor water quality in urban slums caused extensive diarrhea. A new set of infant problems emerged, such as weanling diarrhea, growth stunting, and serious malnutrition—the same problems in the slum areas of Africa and Asia in the twentieth century.

This deteriorating situation was alleviated in the late nineteenth and early twentieth centuries by the development of infant formulations by medical practitioners, the use of tin cans to get the formula to babies who weren't breast-fed, and improved sanitation. The commercial infant formula sector, while viewed today as a negative health force (by those who argue, correctly, that infants should be breast-fed when possible), was important for mothers who had to work and thus couldn't provide breast milk to their children. Around this time, extreme portion control was introduced into the French diet—controls that continue to some extent today and that are a major reason, I argue, for why the French don't get fat. (I explore this in more depth later in this chapter.)

The emergence of chronic diseases such as heart disease and cancer is a recent phenomenon. In the United States and Western Europe a slow increase in heart disease began in the early 1900s, but it wasn't a major health concern until after World War II, when we started to see significant changes in the food and beverage industries and in the way we eat and drink. Of course, there are still some countries, such as Haiti, where only the wealthiest worry about heart disease or cancer, while in other nations few worry about hunger and infectious diseases.

A half-century ago there were fewer than 100 million obese individuals and 7 billion malnourished people. There are now 1.6 billion overweight and obese people in the world, many living with the chronic diseases that contribute to the bulk of deaths worldwide, while there are about 800 million undernourished people. The increase in obesity has been more rapid than the decrease in undernutrition—particularly in the past two decades.

While the origins of the foods we consume date back centuries or more, the role that foods play in our daily lives is a result of more recent agricultural history and the government policies that have shaped our food system. We can think of the food system as the way we produce, transport, and distribute food—it includes all phases in the production of the foods we eat, whether we are talking about corn, wheat, or beef.

When I was a child, my family ate a lot of beef, chicken, corn, and potatoes. We also drank milk. For dessert, we often had whatever fruit happened to be in season. On some occasions my mother would make pie. I rarely had sweets, but I developed a love for them. I couldn't wait for Halloween; I would hoard my candy booty for months. If my mother baked any kind of pastry, I was always trying to eat as much of it as I could. The beef, chicken, corn, potatoes, milk, and even the Halloween candy and homemade pastries were the result of the long and complex history of our country; they were the products of more than a century of government investment and research, of how we nurtured our agricultural system from 1850 onward.

Today, subsidies totaling $30 billion to $50 billion each year are allocated for the production of cheap corn, soybeans, meat, and poultry products. Sugar is a bit different. We used to subsidize its production, but we now protect our sugar producers from cheap imports. Agricultural researchers and the U.S. government worked very hard to develop these cash crops, to increase productivity, and to make them as inexpensive as possible. This extraordinary investment is a major reason why our diet is what it is, both in the United States and in other high-income countries.

Recently, I attended a meeting with organic farmers and others who create local farmers' markets in the United States and Canada. When I asked them if we could create these small markets with their fresh produce in every locality in America, I was given a negative response that used the small town of Pocahontas, Iowa, as an example. The entire commercial enterprise there, including production, irrigation, and transportation, is focused exclusively on corn and soybeans. The farmers would lose a great deal of money if they took acreage out of production to grow vegetables or fruits. Our food system was shaped so that these Iowa farmers could grow just two crops—which produce much of the caloric sweetener and 80 percent of the vegetable oil used in our country. Furthermore, cheap corn, wheat, and soybeans constitute the engine that drives the beef and poultry industries—all of this a major focus of the U.S. government.

Research to provide new types of seeds, fertilizers, and insecticides, and to discover new approaches to cropping, was funded by governments and international agencies. Tax credits and assistance with loans were partially or fully subsidized. It is therefore not surprising that the world price of beef—more than $530 for 220 pounds (100 kilograms) in 1970—declined to less than $190 for the same amount by 1995. The prices of the other commodities discussed above have also declined—the result of systematic institutional assistance and guidance.

U.S. soybean and corn farmers have been selling their crops for less than what it costs to produce them—and that affects, for example, the cost of chicken in the United States. A Tufts University study showed that the broiler industry, including companies like Tyson's and Gold Kist, saved more than $11.25 billion in feed costs for chickens over the eight-year period from 1997 to 2005. The price they paid for feed was 21 percent less than its cost of production. Research by others shows that the subsidies for corn and soybeans have led to reduced costs for pork producers, providing almost $6 billion in extra earnings to Smithfield and the other large ham and pork companies during the same eight-year period.

What at first glance might seem puzzling—farmers taking a loss on their soybean and corn crops—becomes rational when government intervention is taken into account. One result is that over the past three to four decades in the United States, the prices of corn and soybeans have declined while the retail prices of fruits and vegetables have increased. A recent study shows a dramatic decline in real soybean prices from 1975 to 2005 to about 40 percent of their 1975 price. The price of corn declined to about a third of its 1975 price. Given the important role of fructose corn syrup as a sweetener, this means that by extension, sweets and soft drinks have been subsidized—but to a far lesser degree than the meat industry. (Given the tiny costs of sweeteners in beverages, these subsidies are rather trivial.)

So, on one hand, we have much cheaper beef, poultry, corn, soybeans, and sugar. But on the other, this has occurred at the expense of healthy plant foods—particularly fruits and vegetables, whose relative cost is great compared with fats, sugars, and meats in today's marketplaces. The results for all of us—not only in America but around the globe—have been devastating.

As many of us remember from our high school studies, sugar played a very important role in world history. Sugar and spices were the food crops that dominated world trade from the fifteenth to nine-teenth centuries. So important were they, along with codfish, to the emerging global mercantile economy that nations often found them-selves either on the brink of war or at war over them. Sugar and its derivatives—molasses and rum—were the basic currency of trade between Europe and the Americas.

The early history of the Caribbean islands and the American colo-nies in the South revolves around sugar plantations and trade in rum and molasses. By the seventeenth century, the world spice and sugar trades in the Americas, the Caribbean, Asia, and the Far East led to violent clashes over territory, the result of which was that Western powers took over control of production throughout much of the world. The Dutch gave Manhattan to the British in return for the tiny island of Run in the Indonesian Banda Islands, where nutmeg was grown. By far, the English got the worse of the deal in financial terms as the Dutch reaped millions from this spice island—many hundreds of bil-lions of dollars in today's terms. And of course sugar, molasses, and rum played key roles in the American Revolution and in the slave trade.

Government research in the United States began in the nine-teenth century. Sugar research was an immediate focus, and by 1878 it resulted in successful cultivation of sugar beets in Maine and just a year later in the development of the first successful U.S. beet sugar factory, in California. Sugar beets—from whose roots natural sugar is extracted—could grow in the United States much more success-fully than sugarcane, the major sugar plant for the Caribbean and the rest of the world.

And it is no coincidence that the father of modern nutrition and the initiator of the first food initiatives of the agricultural research system, W. O. Atwater, wrote his Ph.D. dissertation on the composi-tion of corn. Presciently, he noted in 1894 that "our diet is one-sided and...we eat too much fat, starch and sugar.... How much harm is done to our health by our one-sided diet? . . . No one can say." The first crosses—a term for new varieties of a crop that were bred—were accomplished with corn in 1881 to increase production. After that, soybeans, livestock, poultry, and dairy production became the foci of much of our funding for agricultural research. In dollar terms, government financial support for crops and animal foods dramatically accelerated after World War II in the United States.

Before the turn of the twentieth century, the U.S. Department of Agriculture was created, the funding of public land grants for colleges to teach agriculture was authorized, the foundation of modern genetics was laid in Gregor Mendel's plant research (1866), government research on animal diseases commenced (1868), a myriad of agricultural cultivation techniques and tools were developed, Aberdeen-Angus bulls were imported from Scotland (the basis for our modern herds of cattle; 1873), payment for the irrigation of arid lands was initiated by the government, milking machines and feed mills were created, the first long-haul shipments of meat in refrigerated boxcars took place (1888)—and I could go on. What is important is that much of the funding focused on key cash crops, on the major staples of the diets of Americans.

Many of the great pushes during this period in terms of capital and technological innovation—and later in the development and expansion of our economy—came from or benefited the agricultural sector. The railways opened up the Midwest, and with that came the ability to ship grain and meat from the farm belt to grain storage sites, dairies, the slaughterhouses of cities like Chicago, and onward to the population centers of the country. Canals were built to move grains. Many technologies were developed during World War II and adapted for farming, including chemicals to manage pest and nutrient issues. Petroleum-based nitrogen fertilizers significantly increased farm productivity.

From 1850 to 1950, the focus on cash crops was a result of politics and preferences of the population. During the nineteenth century, the majority of American workers were farmers. This occupation declined during the twentieth century, but the farmers' voices and roles remained not only in the American economy and political sphere, but also in its psyche. Of course, the most economically important crops received the greatest government support.

In the twentieth century, nutrition became a science. As I mentioned, a change in the way we processed corn caused pellagra, a disease related to niacin (vitamin B$_3$) deficiency. The traditional preparation method for corn used by Native Americans involved treating the corn with lime, an alkali. The lime treatment made niacin nutritionally available, reducing the likelihood of developing pellagra. As corn became commercially milled and used as a staple in the American South, it was no longer soaked with lime. (The milling also removed some protein.) Thousands of poor who relied on a simple diet of milled corn—as corn pone (bread) and other preparations—died from pellagra. But as a result of such nutritional problems, vitamins were discovered.

Scientists also began to understand the importance of animal protein. Several international teams focused on the need for a high animal food diet (beef, dairy, poultry, fish, pork, lamb) as a way to better physical and intellectual development. By the 1940s through the 1960s, competition among countries during the Cold War to produce a strong and healthy citizenry culminated in an overemphasis on animal protein consumption in the diet of Russians. If we thought that Soviet Russia was competing with the United States only on military and space affairs, we were wrong.

Soviet premiers Nikita Khrushchev and Leonid Brezhnev were determined to make the USSR competitive with the United States in space exploration—and in animal food product consumption. One of Khrushchev's major goals was for Russians to eat more meat than

Americans and thus be stronger and more able. This policy was promoted with tens of thousands of posters that idealized the Russian working man with a very muscular arm, flexed with the call to eat more meat.

I worked in Moscow in 1991 as part of the economic team selected by the G-7 to help the former Soviet Union transition to a market economy. I found that Russian nutrition researchers felt their national diet should consist of a much higher level of animal protein and fat than we thought healthy in the West. They didn't care about the financial costs of producing milk, butter, and meat. Nor did they understand the ideas taking hold in the West about reducing both overall calories and saturated fat content to improve health.

The eminent Russian economists and nutritionists whom I met couldn't explain to me *why* this occurred. What did Khrushchev and Brezhnev and their advisers think? I did learn about the devastating health and economic consequences for the citizens of the former Soviet Union. Russian nutritionists were pushed to rationalize a target consumption level of 84 kilograms (almost 185 pounds) of red meat per person per year and to create a scientific basis for this goal. From this came a focus on high levels of animal protein consumption as the key to growth, development, and performance. Saturated fat, cholesterol, total caloric intake, obesity, and other potential negatives were ignored. Only decades later, adults in the former Soviet Union have the highest heart disease rate in the world, are overweight and obese, smoke a great deal, drink extensively, and just aren't healthy.

Of course, medical professionals and nutritionists in the West also thought animal protein was very important for our health. There was a push for agricultural research and promotion of animal products until seminal studies about heart disease led to a major shift in concern among the U.S. health community in the 1960s. Ancel

Keys, a prominent and creative health scholar, showed the relationship between the fat composition of diet and serum cholesterol level. His work led to the early concern about the role of fat in disease. A great amount of heart research followed, over time leading to widespread interest in saturated fat, fat in general, and total cholesterol. For better or worse, his work was the beginning of the end of the scientific rationale for excessive consumption of animal food products. In time, a low-fat diet became the mantra of the West—promoted by the American Heart Association and later by many food companies, physicians, and some nutritionists. In retrospect, we understand that the scientific basis for Keys's work was somewhat flawed and that we overreacted to total fat when we should have focused on the type of fat, the overall quality of our diet, and total calories.

In addition to the misguided emphasis on animal protein, processed food emerged over the last one hundred fifty years. Powdered soups, yeast, substitutes for vanilla and other flavors, bouillon cubes, and the reshaping of processed grains into a vast array of new products resulted from the application of modern chemistry to our food supply. Today, we're awash in highly refined sugar and grains. "Diseases of civilizations" is the term for the diseases caused by removal of vitamins, minerals, and fibers resulting from the processing of rice, wheat, and corn. For example, the famous physicians Denis Burkett and Hugh Trowell felt that colon cancer, diverticulitis, and heart disease were related to the lack of fiber in the Western diet. But while we know that whole grains are very important, and we know about the health risks of consuming too much sugar, refined bread, and refined grain products, we continue to subsidize their production.

The general model of agricultural development that we followed in the United States—first creating a bounty of grain products, then shifting the system to produce animal-source foods—is a basic approach now used for fostering economic development in the poor countries of the world. This model may have served us well at an earlier point in history, but for much of the world it is now beginning to dangerously backfire.

The growth of agriculture is one way in which history has shaped our nutritional lives. A second critical way goes back millions of years. To help us survive as a species, we developed preferences for sweet and fatty foods as well as a dislike of bitterness. Sweet foods provided nutritional balance to our diet, and they helped us survive during periods when animal foods were scarce. Sweet foods also provided the glucose needed to fuel our brains. At this time, however, sugars were only found in fruit. Because there are nine calories of energy in each gram of fat, compared with four calories in each gram of carbohydrate and protein, consuming as much fat as possible would have helped our hunter-gatherer and hominid ancestors to get an adequate amounts of calories. Bitter plants and fruits were often poisonous.

Why are sweets so important? We find that babies instinctively love sweet foods. Not only do newborns react pleasurably to sweets, but in Europe sweetened water is provided to babies when they are given inoculations. The sweets alter the infant's mood and provide a mild anesthetic. Our perception of a sweet taste begins with our tongue, but the brain receptors that are affected by sweets are the same ones affected by cocaine, alcohol, and tobacco. Consumption of sweet foods increases our levels of serotonin, which is believed to play an important role in the regulation of mood, sleep, sexuality, and appetite. (We don't, however, understand a great deal about the full mechanisms.) Perhaps it shouldn't surprise us, then, that the global consumption of caloric sweeteners is at an all-time high and that it's increasing rapidly.

We also know that early hunter-gatherer societies consumed a great amount of fruits and vegetables; in fact, most carbohydrate intake came from these sweeter foods. Studies of food found at archaeological digs, and of the dietary intake of hunter-gatherer societies in this century, such as the !Kung of the Kalahari Desert in southern Africa, have been used by scholars to piece together an understanding of their diet. Many scholars feel that the enormous energy requirements of the human brain led to a need for us to consume high-energy foods. When our brains enlarged from those of our hominid ancestors—three million to seven million years ago—the only sources of sugar were seasonal fruits and berries. Only in the last five thousand years have we learned to derive sugar from sugarcane and other sources such as sugar beets. But to complicate the picture further, some societies—such as pre-1990 China—essentially consumed no sugar, while others—such as Brazil—consumed a great deal. How much of this is genetics and how much has to do with the availability of sweet foods and exposure to the sweet taste is an open question.

Some scholars think that sugar and refined carbohydrates might play a large role in the surge in heart disease (as well as the surge in obesity) over the past decades. John Yudkin, more than any other scholar, deserves credit for pushing forward our understanding of the role of sugar and refined carbohydrates in our diet. But with the American Heart Association's focus on the total fat in our diet—which was based on the work of Ancel Keys—Yudkin's work received scant attention until more recently. As early as the 1950s, Yudkin showed that the link between sugar consumption and coronary heart disease in England was stronger than the link between heart disease and the consumption of saturated fats from animal foods. His work, however, was ignored. In the United States in the past forty years, far more than half of the increase in our daily caloric intake comes from caloric sweeteners, mainly in beverages. I'll discuss this in greater length in the next chapter.

We know that more than 60 percent of us have a very high prefer-
ence for sweetness. The food industry intuitively—or perhaps more
systematically—understands this as well. Thousands of foods in our
supermarkets are sweetened. Does this create a dependency or crav-
ing that increases our consumption of sweetened foods? Do we habit-
uate to sweetness and ultimately require greater and greater levels
of sweetness to satisfy our cravings? While we don't have definitive
answers, we're beginning to understand more about our predilec-
tion for sweet foods. We know, for example, that if we feed sweet
foods to a pregnant woman, the infant will be more likely to eat them
after birth. We also know that if preschoolers eat sweet foods in large
quantities, they'll want more when they are older.

We've seen how our preferences for foods have been shaped by
our evolutionary history, and how—in a very broad sense—our diet
has changed from the Stone Age to the beginning of the Cold War.
What particular trends of the postwar period have conspired to create the fat world of today? In the next chapter, I'll show how the rise
of caloric beverages is related to weight gain and obesity. For the
remainder of this chapter, I'll discuss four trends in the way we eat
that have been detrimental to our health: snacking, weekend eating,
supersizing, and eating away from home.

When I was a child, I ate all my meals with my family. My father
worked one night a week and could not always join us for meals, but
my brother and sister and I always ate dinner together. When I was in
elementary school, I was given a four-ounce container of milk each
day as a snack. When I was really active I might have some fruit or,
on special occasions, a cookie. But for most of my life, I had three
meals a day and only very small snacks.

The members of the Jones family, in contrast, eat different foods, sometimes together, but often at different times. Scott and Linda eat the equivalent of five meals each day. They might snack with their friends after school on a few slices of pizza or a Whopper, and a Pepsi or Coke. (If Linda and her friends are dieting, they drink Diet Coke.) They usually have a late snack of a candy bar or packaged dessert and a Coke. Each snack consists of almost as many calories as breakfast or lunch.

For the Garcia kids, afternoon and evening snacks are soft drinks or fruit juice—to which they add sugar. Bottles of soda wash down cakes from Wal-Mart or Sam's Club. Ana Garcia encourages her children to eat this way; she makes sure there are always soft drinks and pastries on hand. Ana says that it's important to her that her children have the foods she didn't have when she was young.

Incredibly, the Patel children, who live a world away in India, eat the same way. They eat meals with their parents, but their snacks, too, usually consist of a soft drink and something sweet. Noopur, their mother, buys their snack food from a Wal-Mart-inspired mega-supermarket that is owned and run by an Indian company. These cakes and candies—which come from Europe and India and other Asian countries—seemed to me to have been made with condensed sweetened milk or evaporated milk with added sugar; they tasted much sweeter to me than do ours.

In the last fifteen years the size of the snacks we eat—particularly among young adults—has grown rapidly. Today, children and young adults under thirty years of age consume almost one-quarter of their calories from snacks, each of which is about 275 to 300 calories. The one-a-day snacks I ate as a child were less than 100 calories.

Biologically, we eat to fill ourselves with a certain volume of food. "Energy density" is the term for the number of calories in a given weight of food (each 100 grams, for example). Foods with many calories per unit of volume or weight are high energy-dense foods—pizza with extra cheese, or French fries, for example. Carrots, asparagus, pumpkin, greens, apples, and cantaloupe are low in energy density. Higher-energy-density foods contain more fat, protein, and sugar, but less water. The higher the energy density of our foods, the more calories we eat in a meal or as a snack. For example, oily nuts such as pecans or macadamia nuts are about 700 calories per 100 grams, 100 grams of broiled lean steak is around 300 to 400 calories, and broiled codfish is less than 100 calories per 100 grams. (The fact that fats are high in energy density and that studies showed lower-fat diets could reduce heart disease and obesity led to the incorrect argument that reducing dietary fat was *the* way to reduce obesity. We now know that a high-fat, low-carbohydrate diet can also reduce obesity. There are many ways to cut weight if one reduces overall caloric intake.)

My research into U.S. diet trends shows that the energy density of our meals hasn't changed very much, but we have greatly increased the energy density of our snacks, as well as the size and number of snacks per day. Because our ancestors—in an evolutionary sense—needed to fill up on as many calories as possible when they were available as a protection against famine, our bodies likely have been designed to ignore energy density and instead simply encourage us to consume more fat to get more calories.

Snacking on a piece of fruit, or carrots, is far better than eating even the "healthy" snacks, such as the granola and energy bars that we're buying in increasing numbers. Even if so-called healthy snacks don't contain trans fats or gluten, and do contain whole grains, the bottom line is still the calories. Many of these snacks contain lots of sugars and lots of calories per gram of food. Eating several 100- to 200-calorie granola bars is no different from eating many other less healthful snacks. It is important to remember that adding nutrients to junk food still begets junk food. A vitamin C–fortified Coke is still over 100 calories of sugar. Not to mention that because no one in the United States is vitamin C deficient, the benefits of this "healthy" addition to Coke is small or nonexistent. Of course, the beverage and food industries can't advertise that a soft drink or vitamin-enriched beverage or food is healthy, but they certainly allude to it.

A second major difference in eating patterns since the 1950s is the large amount of extra eating and drinking we do on weekends. Growing up, I ate the same foods on the weekend as I did on weekdays. On rare occasions, my mother made waffles or pancakes on Sunday morning. That was the only time our weekend food intake varied from the rest of the week. When my parents visited friends they ate foods similar to what they ate at home, and they drank, at most, one cocktail before dinner.

Bob and Ellen Jones always go out on Friday night. When they are entertaining, or being entertained at dinner, or go out for brunch on Saturdays or Sundays, they drink a lot of wine, or in Bob's case, several beers before switching to wine. When they're drinking, they eat lots of chips, nuts, and other salty and fried snacks. The Garcias often get together with family members for big weekend lunches or dinners. Cesar drinks beer or other alcoholic beverages while Ana only drinks heavily sugared coffee. The children have soft drinks. Fried snacks abound, usually chips, with salsa and guacamole.

Something profound has changed in the way we eat between Friday to Sunday. It's the new three-day weekend. My research shows that the average American adult consumes 115 calories more per day on Friday, Saturday, and Sunday than what they consume on weekdays.

So, we snack every day, and eat more on the weekend, but we've also been supersizing much of what we eat. The movie *Supersize Me,* directed by Morgan Spurlock, makes its point by way of exaggerations—albeit ones that aren't perhaps too far from reality for some of us.

During the 1970s, a marketing director of McDonald's Corporation, David Wallerstein, determined that consumers would buy more of a food or beverage item sold in larger sizes; furthermore he argued and showed that the costs for the extra food weren't large. Thereafter, larger sizing for a cheaper marginal cost became the mantra at McDonald's. During the same period, through the innovative leadership of a McDonald's franchisee, the company began packaging foods together into value meal combinations. It was a tidy way to get customers to spend and eat more.

The value meal is similar to a fixed price meal, which began in France and packages a number of foods together to give the customer the sense he is getting more for his money. By preparing larger quantities of the same foods, the restaurant is usually more efficient, resulting in a lower cost for packaged-together foods. But for the customer, the end effect is like supersizing: with supersizing pricing, we get more calories per dollar—we get a larger portion and thus we eat more.

Together, supersizing and value meals caused a seismic shift in American eating habits.

Supersizing at McDonald's was copied by other companies, and soon value meals that promoted supersizing became a clear direction for the entire industry. While the history of this bellwether period—who did what, and who copied whom—remains to be written, it is clear that the entire fast-food industry changed during the 1980s and 1990s. Meanwhile, the packaged-food industry was doing the same: larger portion sizes for junk food and soft drinks became the mode of sales promotion.

Increased portion sizes, particularly for energy-dense dishes such as French fries, has been an important force behind our increased food intake over the past decade. The same is true for high-calorie beverages such as Pepsi. If you went to McDonald's in the 1950s, you bought an eight-ounce soft drink. Today, the size of the smallest drink there is twelve ounces—and there are many larger sizes. Remarkably, however, McDonald's has recently been reducing many of its portion sizes while its competitors—with no apparent concern for the health of their customers—are introducing ever larger burgers and drinks. (I discuss this in depth in Chapter 6.)

In one study, a group of anthropologists used in-depth case studies to examine how the food consumption both at home and in restaurants was affected by the introduction of McDonald's in Asian countries, including China, Taiwan, and South Korea. They discovered that restaurants and homemakers learned to mimic some elements of how fast-food chains process food, including serving larger drinks and food portions. The manner in which the McDonald's approach to selling food penetrates a culture's food byways is complex and will never be fully understood. However, studies confirm that the effects are profound. For instance, children seem to want to consume more food that is held without utensils—i.e., finger food—and frying, as well, has become more popular.

Some of the effects of fast food on our eating habits occur quickly. Soon after their first McDonald's and KFC meals, Scott and Linda Jones frequently told their parents how they loved fast-food restaurants. They asked to be taken there as often as possible. They also started to push their mother to buy larger portions of the prepared take-out foods that she feeds them at home. Slowly, the norm for what was a dinner at home—a serving of pizza, or pasta, or a hamburger—began to approach the portion sizes served at their favorite fast-food restaurants. And it's not only the Joneses. I studied the food intake of Americans from 1977 to the last decade. By the end of the study, serving sizes of French fries and hamburgers consumed at home were 30 percent larger than in fast-food restaurants. The serving sizes of Mexican dishes and pizza were equal to those in fast-food restaurants.

Trends in France offer a compelling counterpoint to the supersizing of the world. The French have been less likely to supersize their diet than other high-income industrialized countries. A rigorous discipline of weighing and portioning the foods of each meal evolved over time in France, and may explain why, despite their wine and rich diets, the French can eat so well and not get as fat as others.

Beginning in 1904, but with its roots in the development of infant formula by French physicians in the 1880s, the French government played a strong role in supporting the "puericulture" movement—the care of a child before and after birth. They passed a national Public Health Act and established clinics to teach young mothers portion control. This system of advocacy educated mothers about feeding their babies; it focused not only on what to feed infants but also on the appropriate quantities. The government regulated the foods that schools could serve, and later the food advertising during children's television programming.

At first, puericulture clinics were located in all communities. Puericulture practitioners guided mothers on the kinds of milk and food to give children, but they were also very concerned about overfeeding. In fact, they encouraged underfeeding. Famous gynecologists and pediatricians promoted the puericulture concept, and when a period of rapid decline in infant mortality followed, the movement received a lot of the credit. By far the most effective and well-known advocate of this approach to child feeding was Augusta Moll-Weiss, a Frenchwoman who wrote books about home economics that were considered definitive. For Moll-Weiss, the key to good childhood health was parental control of the table.

Mothers were taught to weigh their children's portions and to control them carefully. Older children were forced to eat at regular mealtimes and consume modest portions—no seconds and no snacks. Virtually every French child was raised based on Moll-Weiss's advice. Eventually, these children had families of their own, and the cycle of portion control and good eating habits was perpetuated down the generations and throughout French society. To paraphrase the popular best seller, *French Women Don't Get Fat*: Yes, French women eat fat, but they also eat fewer calories. This is their secret. Their approach to eating well and staying slender is related to portion-size control.

Another "secret" of good French habits was revealed when a psychologist and student of eating behavior looked at the amount of time the French spend eating versus their American counterparts. It turns out that French eating occasions extend over a much longer period of time. And as we know, eating slowly rather than rushing down our food will make us feel full sooner, while we are consuming less.

And yet, with the advent of fast-food chains and new media, French traditions are breaking down. Portion controls are declining, as is the average length of time spent at the table. But even as more Frenchmen find themselves fighting battles of the bulge, boundary setting continues. Basically, the state still regulates the excesses of modern life. You won't find Coca-Cola in a French middle school, for example. Is it possible to replicate the French story of government intervention and its paternalistic, authoritarian way of treating parents in regard to the care of their children? South Korea tried something similar; I'll discuss this in depth in Chapter 7.

Why should portion controls concern us? Research demonstrates that larger portion sizes do affect what we eat. We don't know if this is a result of visual cues, socialization, or other factors, but people in a number of countries around the world now feel that larger amounts are normal, or even "appropriate."

Research also shows that, essentially, we'll eat as much as we're served. In particular, Brian Wansink's creative research has shown how profoundly we're tricked when it comes to eating and portion sizes. The research is quite convincing and may relate to the feast-or-famine seasonality of the hunter-gatherer diet of the Paleolithic era. Studies show that when we're given larger plates or bowls of food, we consume more; when we are given larger portions with identical amounts of calories per 100 grams, we consume more; and even with bottomless bowls, we consume more.

In terms of where we eat our food and who cooks it, the changes in the last half-century are nothing short of revolutionary. For thousands of years only travelers ate meals away from home. Food prepared at home was the source of almost all of the world's calories.

In my early years, my family ate out in restaurants one to three times a year. On a few occasions while attending elementary school, I was allowed to eat lunch at school, but otherwise all my meals were eaten at home or at relatives' homes. When I attended high school, which was miles from our house, my siblings and I took sandwiches to school. I would often have an after-school snack at my grandmother's house or at my friends' homes, if I was playing there. The thought of eating daily at a restaurant was foreign to people in the 1950s. Even when I was in college in the 1960s, eating out was a big deal—something we did on Sunday night, on a date, or for a special occasion.

As I've mentioned, the Jones family eats out a lot. Bob eats out every day. Ellen frequently has lunch at the local diner with her fellow teachers or, less often, brings something with her to eat in the teachers' lounge. The children's meals at school usually consist of fast food served in the cafeteria. The Garcia family is typical of many

Mexican families in California in that they always eat at home. In Chapel Hill, North Carolina, where I now live, there are about twenty thousand Hispanic residents. In contrast to the Garcias, about half of the Hispanics in Chapel Hill are single men and they never cook; they always eat out, usually at one of the little *tiendas* that are found around town—most of which have small kitchens that turn out home-made tacos and enchiladas—or in the small Mexican restaurants.

Incredibly, more than half of the money Americans spend on food today is for meals consumed away from home. That doesn't count how much we spend on food prepared at grocery stores that we take home to eat. Children and teenagers still get over two-thirds of their calories at home, but this is rapidly declining. Of course, fast food is a large component of our away-from-home eating; but "slower" fast-food restaurants such as Panera Bread and Chipotle Mexican Grill provide fast service without the preprepared food, which is healthier and tends to be consumed more slowly.

Before moving on to a discussion of how beverages are contributing to our overweight world, I want to briefly address one last change in how we eat—the rise of "healthy" food fads, from superfoods such as pomegranates, blueberries, sour cherries, and acai berries to organic fruits, vegetables, and meats. Most of these foods are not as beneficial—if they're beneficial at all—as claimed. In some cases, eating more of these foods because we think they're healthy could lead to weight gain. (I'm focusing here on the nutritional composition of these organic foods, not addressing the matters of pesticides and hormones, which do concern many of us.)

In general, the nutritional values of organic food are not much greater than that of nonorganic food. Grass-fed or range-fed animals and poultry are an exception with their lower fat content and healthier set of fats, and organic foods are likely to have fewer pesticides, in the case of fruits and vegetables, and fewer other additives, in the case of animal-based foods. We're all familiar with the foods that are marketed to us as something that will make us healthier by, say, reducing heart disease. Almost no superfoods will do this. In fact, only a few foods, such as chocolate, have been tested for their effects on humans. But even in the case of chocolate, it's unclear whether eating a tiny piece will lead to health benefits or whether you need to consume 200 to 300 calories per day, which would likely lead to weight gain. Soon we'll have chewing gum—and many foods—with added antioxidants. Will these vitamin-laced foods be of any benefit? Like consuming enough dark chocolate to lower one's blood pressure, consuming these elements in these foods could have more negative effects—weight gain, for example—than purported benefits.

In fact, antioxidant vitamins, which dozens of these foods and beverages are noted to be rich in, are not linked to increased longevity and the many other benefits often promised by the food industry. Extensive reviews of the benefits of vitamins A, E, and C, beta-carotene, and selenium show just the opposite. One study found that "treatment with beta-carotene, vitamin A, and vitamin E may increase mortality, while the potential roles of vitamin C and selenium on mortality need further study." In this study, these antioxidants were taken directly—that is, not as part of a food. Will these antioxidants improve our health when they're added to our food? We'll have to wait and see, but my personal bet is that they'll be less harmful than taking excessive antioxidants directly, but hardly good enough for you to justify eating more of this next-generation superfood.

2

We Are What We Drink

The way we eat today—in large portions, away from home, with lots of energy-dense snacks in between meals, maybe with a superfood thrown in here or there—is only part of the reason why so many of us are overweight. Perhaps nothing has contributed more to our weight gain than the clash between our drinking habits and our biology.

Our genus, *Homo*, separated from other hominids between two million and three million years ago. Our species, *Homo sapiens*, appeared between two hundred thousand and one hundred thousand years ago. But it's likely that until wine and beer were invented—about eleven thousand years ago—we didn't drink anything other than water or breast milk. Our hunter-gatherer predecessors drank breast milk for the first few years of their lives, and after that only water.

But during the last century we've seen huge changes in the kinds of beverages consumed throughout the world—changes our biology isn't prepared for. Imagine what would have happened to a hunter-gatherer if his or her hunger was satiated by drinking water. He or she wouldn't feel the need to forage for food, and wouldn't have stored essential body fat for times of famine. It's obvious that if water consumption alleviated our hunger pangs we, as a species, might not have survived. Another way of looking at this is that those who survived did not cut their food intake after drinking. And for us today the implications are clear—we drink a lot of our calories, but we don't cut our food intake as a result. Recent studies confirm this. We can have a sixteen-ounce bottle of Coke or three beers before dinner—and not eat any less because of it.

The relatively recent addition of caloric beverages to our diet—shown in the illustration below—provides a sense of the role of beverages in the obesity pandemic. Compared with the millions of years during which we evolved into *Homo sapiens*, the span of time in which we've been consuming caloric beverages has been very short.

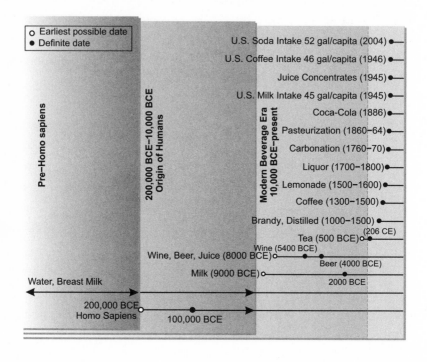

Our genes take a long time to respond to such changes—we're living in a rapidly changing world but with genes adapted to an earlier period.

Before we examine some of the new high-calorie beverages of the past few decades, let's take a look at the brief history of the beverages that have been around for a while—water, milk, coffee, tea, beer, and wine—and the roles that they play in our lives today.

Water is the basis of life for all mammals. Before we developed agriculture, water was rarely contaminated. Then, with agriculture and subsequent urbanization, feces (animal and human) and other contaminants created health problems related to water consumption. Pathogens periodically led to outbreaks of cholera and dysentery; more recently, toxic chemicals have caused problems.

Today, bottled water has been the savior in countries where public sources of water are contaminated. Elsewhere, the rise of designer bottled waters has been a steady and healthful trend. Nonetheless, the disposal of these plastic water bottles has become a legitimate environmental concern, revealing how the positive goals of different groups can collide. Some municipalities are attempting to ban water bottles, and a *New York Times* editorial in August 2007 spoke against bottled water. But I think it's inappropriate to single out one source of plastic bottles without condemning other—much less healthy—sources of plastic bottles.

People have been conditioned to carry bottled beverages around—and we need that to be water. It would be better for schools and other public and private facilities to sell water rather than caloric beverages, such as soft drinks, fruit juice, whole milk, energy drinks, and heavily sugared teas. Today, the need to have safe, clean, accessible water is, of course, not limited to the United States. Mexicans, for example, drink as much, if not more, soft drinks than we do. The typical portion sizes in Mexico are one and two liters, as opposed to our sixteen-ounce portions (about a half-liter). Consequently, obesity levels in Mexico are as high as those in the United States. Mexicans don't have safe tap water, so they need to have access to bottled water as an alternative to sodas.

In a fast-paced society, we need people to think first of water—wherever they are. Too many Americans will drink Red Bull, Pepsi, or sugared vitamin waters—all with excessive calories. Drinking water, whether it comes from a faucet or a bottle, is an easy step we can all take toward better health. Bottled water should not be pitted against tap water, however. This is a false choice. We should talk about the essential need we all have to consume more water. And of course, we should push for the complete recycling of bottles and other containers. But we shouldn't single out the healthiest beverage we have—we shouldn't ignore other beverage containers and take-out food containers that are equally harmful to the environment but which contain less healthy beverages and foods. They are equal scourges to the Earth's future—and their health benefits are clearly not as important as those of water.

In the West, we tend to think milk, from cows, sheep, or goats, is critical to life. However, animal milk is a recent addition to our diet. Historians haven't been able to definitively determine when milk was first consumed. The earliest reliable record of dairy products is a tablet left by a Sumerian farmer in approximately 4000 BCE, which details the size of a herd and tells us of cheese and butter production. Of course, this doesn't guarantee that the farmer drank milk.

The consumption of milk is very interesting from an evolutionary standpoint. The enzyme lactase is required to be able to digest the lactose in milk, and most of the people in the world lose this enzyme after they're weaned from their mother's breast. Genetic and archaeological research has found that the first known population of adults to be fully able to ingest milk was the Funnel Beaker culture, which flourished five thousand to six thousand years ago in central Europe. Today, the descendants of these people—the Swedes, Danes, and other north-central Europeans—have the enzyme lactase and thus can digest milk without the side effects experienced by people who are lactose intolerant. Geneticists have recently shown that as we move away from northern and central Europe toward southern Europe and the Middle East, people don't possess the correct genetic makeup to break down lactose. However, some exciting studies have found several populations in eastern Africa that also possess the lactase gene. Complex genetic analyses suggest that the gene mutations in eastern Africa arose between 2,700 and 6,800 years ago. This is one of several recent discoveries that have revealed how rapidly our genes can change at the local level as a result of environmental pressures. It's clear that northern and central Europeans and eastern Africans needed essential nutrients from milk and thus developed the ability to digest it. Americans who descended from northern and central European peoples are today some of the small subsets of the world population who have adequate amounts of the enzyme lactase. Most American blacks came from areas in Africa where milk was not consumed, and thus are lactose intolerant, as are many Asians who have immigrated to the United States.

Until the beginning of the nineteenth century, milk consumption was limited even for lactose-tolerant peoples. Before the French scientist Louis Pasteur invented in the 1860s the process we now call pasteurization, which uses heat to destroy microorganisms, milk could transmit diseases such as cholera, polio, anthrax, scarlet fever, bovine tuberculosis, and botulism. By the 1900s, milk had become much more popular in the United States and Europe, and producers made huge advances in handling, processing, and distributing pasteurized milk to places far from its source.

More recent developments in heat treatment, and the invention of a now widely used alternative to pasteurization called ultra-high temperature, or UHT—in which milk is raised to a temperature of 138°C (280°F) for about two seconds—have allowed the distribution and storage of milk without refrigeration. As UHT-treated milk does not require refrigeration, it has become increasingly used in Europe, Asia, and Africa. It's very safe—but it doesn't taste as good to the American palate as does fresh milk.

Milk consumption patterns are at present changing rapidly in the United States. We are tailoring milk to compete with sweetened beverages; there are an increasing number of new flavored and sweet milk products, including chocolate and strawberry milk, in stores and vending machines. These sugary and higher-fat milk products are no better than other sugared beverages; the adverse effect of sugar offsets the nutritional benefits of milk.

Beer was one of the most common beverages consumed before the modern era. The Sumerians are generally considered to have produced the first beer around 8000 BCE, but the Egyptians were the first ones to mass-produce it by breaking bread into water and allowing it to ferment. The introduction of hops to beer by Jews in early Babylon helped prevent spoilage, but it didn't gain widespread use until the sixteenth century, when the extended shelf life of beer helped increase its popularity.

Beer is now the most widely consumed alcoholic beverage in the world. It has been a more important beverage in Europe than in the United States. Much of the reason for this goes back to the Temperance movement in the United States, to Christian teachings related to abstinence from alcohol, and to the way Americans culturally have treated alcohol. It's not uncommon to see a small child in Belgium or Germany drinking beer with a meal, and the same holds in France, Spain, and Italy for wine. In the United States, we have a legal drinking age of twenty-one. I think it's clear that the restrictive manner in which the United States treats alcoholic beverages plays a role in the self-destructive patterns in which teens and college students consume alcohol.

Wine originated in the Middle East, where today, ironically, alcohol is banned in many countries. The earliest evidence of winemaking from domesticated grapes comes from Iran, between 5400 and 5000 BCE. Like the first beer, the first wine was likely made by accident. Some juice could have escaped from grapes stored in vessels and natural yeasts would have produced alcohol in two or three days. Once discovered, wine spread rapidly throughout Mesopotamia. Grapevines have been reported in Egypt, Greece, and elsewhere in the Mediterranean region at about the same time—by 3000 BCE. The Romans, after conquering the Greeks, became great wine enthusiasts, drinking it at all meals but usually diluting it with water. Wine consumption spread with the Roman Empire's expansion.

After the collapse of Rome, wine's place in Christian rituals helped sustain production through the instability of the Dark Ages. Monasteries protected and refined the art of winemaking during a period when vines were difficult to maintain in Europe because of social unrest. In the Middle East and North Africa, winemaking was vanishing because of the advance of Islam. Eventually, Islam drove winemaking out of its ancestral home in Iran and Iraq, but European expansion during the last five centuries carried wine production throughout the world. Sharia (Islamic law) prohibits intoxicants, whether alcohol, drugs, or fermented juices. Europeans brought wine-making to the Americas, starting in Mexico and going southward to Peru, Chile, and Argentina. Early settlers in North America found their European grapes being attacked by root-eating aphids, so they began producing wine from native varieties.

The last century—particularly the last decade—has seen a major resurgence of wine consumption. In fact, total alcohol intake, mostly from wine and beer, increased fourfold in the United States between 1965 and 2002. Today, the average American adult consumes over 100 calories a day from alcohol. Research shows that in the United States we consume much of our alcohol in a three-day weekend—Friday to Sunday—whereas in Europe, alcohol intake occurs pretty much over the entire week. During this new three-day weekend, Americans consume 115 calories more per day than they do Monday through Thursday.

Tea is the world's most commonly consumed beverage—second only to water. But this wasn't always the case. In fact, tea wasn't always a drink. Today, we get our caffeine from beverages. In many parts of the world going back to the Stone Age, people chewed leaves, seeds, and bark to get caffeine, and to relieve fatigue. Only with the discovery of tea was caffeine first documented as coming from a beverage. The earliest consumers of tea—in Thailand, Burma, Assam, and southwest China—chewed or cooked the leaves of the tea plant, *Camellia sinensis*. Tea didn't reach Europe until the seventeenth century as a result of the East Asian trade. The British adapted to tea in a most serious way and learned to boil it in water independent of earlier tea drinkers.

There are many legends about the origins of tea. What is clear is that it was consumed first in China around 2700 BCE, and was developed either by servants of a Chinese emperor or by the emperor himself. The first book about tea was written in China in 780 by Lu Yum, known as the sage of tea; this work is considered the classic study on the cultivation, preparation, and consumption of tea.

Iced tea was introduced at the 1893 Chicago World's Fair, where a U.S. concessionaire sold it and made a great deal of money. Tea bags were invented in the United States a few years later. We're in a new kind of tea revolution in the United States. Snapple, Arizona Tea, and other higher-calorie versions started this trend. Today, bottled green teas are the rage; they're marketed as having all kinds of health benefits. Green tea itself is currently the leader of this fad, but others could take over. The new "calorie-burning" beverages such as Enviga, which began to be promoted nationally in early 2007, will fuel this tea trend as they derive key ingredients from green tea. While many alternative-health proponents such as Dr. Andrew Weil promote green tea consumption as of great benefit to our health, beverage scholars I've worked with don't see this research as being convincing. A new generation of research is under way to more carefully determine if there are health benefits from green tea intake. Most green tea studies to date are on mice or involve tiny numbers of humans, but I expect this will change over the next five years. We are beginning to see studies on daily tea intake providing some protection against heart attacks and strokes.

Coffee is a relatively recent addition to our beverage lineup. In about the ninth century, coffee use originated in Ethiopia and/or across the Red Sea in Yemen. First the beans were simply eaten. Roasted beans and brewed coffee came probably from Yemen during the late fourteenth or early fifteenth century. Muslim rituals eventually came to include coffee. Long before Europeans even considered drinking coffee, coffeehouses became a major meeting place in Islamic society. For a religion that prohibited alcohol intake, caffeine-containing coffee was a very popular beverage. Coffee drinking came to Europe in the 1600s and rapidly spread among the elite classes. With the progress of colonialism, coffee cultivation expanded to the Caribbean and South America.

The upswing in global commerce that began after World War II has fueled an international renaissance in coffee consumption. Northern Europeans, for the most part, always consumed very high-quality coffee—unlike the rest of the world. The United States, in particular, drank weak, diluted coffee in the first eighty years of the twentieth century. While we tend to think that Starbucks led Americans' shift toward drinking higher-grade, stronger coffee, the picture is much more complex. Our nation's understanding and consumption of coffee were pushed forward by the now legendary Alfred Peets, who founded the eponymous coffee shop and company in Berkeley in 1966; Saul Zabar, the founder of Zabar's in New York City; the nation of Colombia, with its huge advertising campaign featuring their invented coffee grower, the mustached Juan Valdez; and other, lesser known coffee zealots.

Starbucks was a latecomer to the revolution. In the 1960s, three friends—Jerry Baldwin, Gordon Bowker, and Zev Siegl—spent the summer in Europe. They loved the dark European roasted coffees. By 1970, then in their late twenties, they all landed in Seattle. Two were unhappy teachers and one a writer. In search of good coffee, they went to Vancouver to buy beans. Then Gordon Bowker got the idea of opening a shop in Seattle. They had tasted Alfred Peets's coffee beans from Berkeley. Zev Siegl went there and met with Peets, who was very generous and helped them in many ways. Before long, Siegl was working in Peets's Berkeley store to learn more about the trade. The trio opened their first Starbucks coffee shop in Seattle.

Peets provided the roasted beans and helped them get the equipment they needed. Their first stores were designed to look like Peets's coffee mecca in Berkeley. They stayed small until they were joined by Howard Schultz, a very sharp marketer and businessman.

Schultz first traveled to Seattle in 1981 as a sales rep for a Swedish coffeemaker to check out the popular coffee-bean store called Starbucks. He loved what he saw, especially the dedication to educating the public about the wonders of coffee. He decided he wanted to work with Bowker, Siegl, and Baldwin. Schultz tried to convince them to hire him to direct their marketing. It took a year, but in 1982 Schultz became director of marketing and operations for Starbucks.

Schultz visited Milan and saw espresso served everywhere. He went back to Starbucks and tried to get them to do the same. They refused, so Schultz quit and started his own coffee-bar business, called Il Giornale. It was successful, and a year later Schultz bought Starbucks for $3.8 million. In the 1990s he began to expand rapidly. The rest is history. The company really exploded after a public stock offering in 1992. Starbucks changed the way Americans view coffee. Gone were the days of instant coffee.

Schultz took the company international in the mid-1990s. Starbucks's U.S. growth may have slowed, but its global growth certainly has not. As I walk the streets of Beijing, I see more and more Starbucks. They plan to open thousands of stores here and lead the Chinese from tea intake to coffee consumption. As my Chinese colleague and president of the Chinese Nutrition Society, Ge Keyou, told me recently: people want variety. I was lamenting the caloric increases that will come to China from Starbucks's high-calorie coffee, but he saw this as providing choices that the people wanted. Of course, he is correct—but so am I. If Starbucks were to shift from two percent milk and optional skim milk to offering only skim milk, the cost of this kind of progress would be much less.

———————

The history of fruit and vegetable juices is much more limited than that of the beverages discussed above, although coconut and others juices go back to the period before Christ. Fruit juices were used to protect sailors from scurvy in the 1800s. The mass production of fruit juice, the use of pasteurization, and the development of juice concentrates were accomplished in the last one hundred years. Concentrated juice was invented during World War II to help provide sustenance to combat troops. Oversupplies of fruit juice and huge freezes in the 1950s in southern Florida that spoiled the direct consumption of oranges led to larger-scale production operations and the promotion of both fruit-juice concentrate and mixed fruit juices in the United States. Today, the consumption of fruit juice is ubiquitous in Mexico and Australia. In Australia, fruit juice is the major caloric beverage consumed by children and adolescents, and in Mexico for some age groups the consumption of fruit juice is on par with that of soft drinks.

As a child, I drank milk and tap water. I began the day with a small glass of orange juice, but milk and water were the norm. I washed down my lunch with about four fluid ounces of milk. There were functioning water fountains everywhere. At home, my father drank hot tea for breakfast, sometimes with a little sugar added, and my mother drank coffee throughout the day, also with a little sugar. And maybe, on a weekend or for a special occasion, my parents had a drink or a glass of wine. None of us thought this diet bland—or could have imagined all the choices to come.

In contrast, the adults in the Garcia and Jones families drink alcohol all the time. Their homes are stocked with soft drinks, fruit drinks, coffee (drunk with a lot of sugar), and fruit juices. Today, the average American gets over 400 calories a day from beverages.

When I go to Nabenchauk, a lower-income Mayan village in Chiapas, Mexico, where my former partner is doing research, I'm amazed at the street stands filled with soft drinks—Mexico consumes more soft drinks per capita than any other country in the world. In India, the situation is different but the net result is much the same. The Patels seldom drink water because the water in their village is polluted. Instead, they drink thoroughly boiled tea to which they add a lot of heavy water-buffalo milk and sugar; their tea is very high in fat and calories. They also drink a lot of milk and eat a great deal of yogurt. Dairy-based beverages in India have about 4 to 10 percent more fat than the whole milk we drink in the United States. And the Patels add a lot of sugar or ghee to their yogurt beverages, amounting to hundreds of extra calories per day. Since they don't grow or eat any vegetables, they need to drink more fluids to stay alive and function. In all, they drink beverages with even more calories than the beverages the Joneses and Garcias drink.

When I lived in India, I knew I would become sick if I drank the water—and I did, often. When I could, I'd drink a Coca-Cola, which was omnipresent and easy to find on any street corner. This is why Mexicans drink so many canned and bottled beverages—they are safe. You don't get the bacteria in Coke, Pepsi, or any other bottled beverage that you do in unsafe water; bottled water is also popular in such a setting. In government schools in Mexico, there is no access to clean water. Without functioning water fountains or water dispensers, what are children going to do except bring bottled beverages to school? And with bottled water the same price as soft drinks, what child would not prefer a sugary beverage? The same is true for most adults. Why buy water when it is the same price as other, tastier beverages?

We all have an intuitive understanding of why we drink. We need a certain amount of water daily to survive. Blood is mostly water, and our muscles, lungs, and brain all contain a lot of water. Our bodies need water to regulate body temperature and to transport nutrients to our organs, to transport oxygen to our cells, to remove waste, and to protect our organs. We'll die if we go more than two or three days without water. We drink more now than we did a decade or two ago—but not because we are more active and need more water.

A former student of mine is dedicated to studying water and its effects on human health. Research that we've done together on water and dieting in women shows that increased water intake is linked with reduced energy intake, weight, risk of diabetes, and cardiovascular problems. I'm also currently involved in three randomized controlled trials involving adults and children; we want to know if the link between water and health is robust. My sense is that we'll show not only that water is important for replacing caloric beverages, but that there are additional health benefits to water as well.

Consider the day of an average American. Surprisingly, some Americans start their day with soft drinks. I studied food patterns at breakfast and found that about 5 percent of Americans drank soft drinks despite the early hour, a figure that has increased since the study was conducted. This, of course, is the exception: most of us drink milk, tea, or coffee with some juice for breakfast. Others drink huge amounts of juice—equal to several cans of soda in terms of calories. About 10 percent will also have a sweetened latte or a soft drink later in the morning. Afternoon, dinner, and evening beverages are most likely soft drinks, wine, beer, or, possibly, water. The average American adult drinks sugared beverages about two and a half times a day. More than 450 of a person's daily calories come from beverages—40 percent from soft drinks or fruit juices and 20 percent from alcohol.

We Are What We Drink

Today we get twice as many calories from beverages as we did in 1965. In the United States we didn't drink a lot of fruit juice until the late 1950s, when a freeze in Florida resulted in a huge supply of shriveled oranges that were used for juice. Until then, the big caloric beverage was whole milk, and a little alcohol. I often encounter the perception that Americans drank a lot of beer or cocktails in the 1950s—but this isn't true except for small subpopulations of higher-income Americans. On average we consumed much less alcohol in the 1950s than today. About the time of World War II, we drank mostly water, tea, coffee, a limited amount of beer and hard alcohol, and whole milk; our calorie intake per day from beverages was between 100 and 200 calories. By 2002, we more than doubled our intake of caloric beverages. From 1965 to 2002, over two-thirds of this increase (and half of our total calories from beverages) was due to fruit juices and soft drinks. Water consumption, on the other hand, hasn't changed. In 1989, we drank about five glasses (or forty fluid ounces) of water a day, and we drink the same amount today. (Of course, we drink more bottled water now and less water from the tap, but water is water.)

How we drink as well as what we drink today is a result of major advances in food processing, distribution, and aggressive marketing campaigns on the part of the beverage industry that began around the turn of the twentieth century and accelerated after World War II. Around the world, from about 1990 on, the beverage industry has been successful in marketing the idea of always drinking: drink when you're active, drink when you're resting and relaxing, drink when you want to party. Speaking to the explosion in the variety of beverages is the Coca-Cola website, which states that the "Coca-Cola Company offers nearly four hundred products in more than two hundred countries (including eighty brands in the United States alone) to hydrate, energize, nourish, relax or enjoy every drop of life. And, we're always introducing new beverages to meet your changing demands."

Soft drinks were added to the beverage pantheon, rather ironically, with the intention of making us healthier. Waterborne pathogens have been the scourge of mankind for millennia. Because carbonation kills many kinds of bacteria, early beverage makers focused on producing naturally carbonated water, mainly from famous European spas. Carbonation techniques involving chalk and acid were developed in the 1760s, resulting in a beverage sometimes called "soda water" as bicarbonate of soda was used to create carbonation. And even in the United States well into the 1950s, carbonated water made with spritzer bottles was still very common.

Dr Pepper, first made in 1885 in Waco, Texas, was the first major soft drink in the United States. As with other soft drinks, its formula was invented by a pharmacist, Charles Alderton, who was working for Wade B. Morrison. The son of British immigrants, Alderton was an M.D. who decided to work as a pharmacist. He moved to Waco and joined Morrison in his Old Corner Drug Store, where he developed a combination of fruit extracts that he poured from the drugstore soda fountain. It sold very well. At first customers called it "Doc Alderton's drink." Morrison renamed it "Dr Pepper" after a friend of his, Dr. Charles Pepper.

The beginning of Coca-Cola is similar. It was invented in 1886 by Dr. John Pemberton, a pharmacist from Atlanta, Georgia, who wanted to develop the ultimate medicine and perfect drink. He concocted it in his backyard, and marketed it as "the valuable tonic and nerve stimulant properties of the coca plant and cola nuts"—ergo, the hyphenate "Coca-Cola," which was created by Pemberton's book-keeper. Before Pemberton died, a few years later, he sold most of the business to Asa Candler, who eventually acquired complete control and incorporated the company that is selling beverages around the world today.

As part of their effort to create strong identification with their product, Coca-Cola turned soft drinks into a big business. During World War II, Coca-Cola worked closely with the U.S. War Department to provide free Coke to GIs. As a result of a lobbying campaign, they were allowed to break sugar ration rules and to create Coke plants in European countries with the support of the government. The U.S. Army allowed Coke staff members to be designated "technical observers," sent overseas at government expense to set up bottling plants behind the lines. Interestingly, this included being allowed to operate Coca-Cola plants in Hitler's Germany. Pepsi didn't get special access to sugar rations or any of the other privileges afforded Coca-Cola.

Soda is here to stay. But America has always been a restless nation, and our penchant for new foods and beverages is no exception. One year, it's a certain kind of red wine that everyone is drinking (such as the Merlot craze a few years back); another year, the new "it" beverage might be Snapple or Arizona Tea, or more recently, Vitamin Water. Today, the push is toward "healthier" functional beverages, including energy drinks like Red Bull, calorie-burning drinks like Enviga, and new waters that claim to enhance your complexion. The next generation will include fruit juices and dairy products that even promise to provide beauty. Are any of these newfangled beverages really healthful? Are they worth their eye-popping prices?

I hadn't heard of energy drinks until 1997. Then I suddenly saw Red Bull all over the United States, Europe, and Asia. Today, in U.S. convenience stores it's the third-best-selling product. The creation and marketing of Red Bull is a remarkable story.

In 1982, Dietrich Mateschitz got the idea for Red Bull from a Thai beverage called Krating Daeng that he drank at the elite Mandarin Hotel in Hong Kong. (A different story, told in *The Economist*, is that Mateschitz drank Krating Daeng in 1982 when he visited Thailand, and discovered that the drink helped cure his jet lag.) He formed the Red Bull company in 1984 and started selling Red Bull Energy Drink to the Austrian market in 1987. A lot happened between 1984 and 1987. First, the Austrian equivalent of the FDA wouldn't approve Red Bull. Then the company's marketing researchers told him the drink was no good, that taste tests showed consumers didn't like it. So, here was a drink that needed to create an *image*; it needed to be *experienced*, and it needed to establish an *attitude*. It was not a pharmaceutical, but rather something to be sampled. Red Bull ditched traditional TV and radio marketing and began to provide samples and to sponsor events.

It was painful to get approval for Red Bull's ingredients in Austria and other countries. It took five years to gain permission for export into Germany, Red Bull's second market but its true beginning. Speculation about the reasons for its illegality in Germany was critical to its success. Many called it speed in a can, a legal drug. Some thought of one ingredient, taurine (an organic acid used in infant formula), as coming from bulls' testicles and a source of sexual prowess. The rumors began. When Red Bull was finally approved and launched in Germany, moms there united to have it banned. This was the godsend it needed. It became cool, it became the symbol of defiance of authority, and it reached a tipping point. No matter what happened in the future, this cool, "with it" attitude carried forward. Journalists called it "liquid cocaine," but of course the rumors of Red Bull's potentially dangerous effect just helped sell the drink. And the company's sponsorship of events enhanced its cachet. (Red Bull has purchased two Formula One teams and its own football team, which it named Red Bull Salzburg.)

It's difficult to sort out how much of Red Bull's success is attributable to its actual physical effects, how much to its image as a counterculture drink, and how much to its message of energy and stimulation. But wherever you see it marketed, these are the themes. It used its initial cultlike following to grow to global proportions in just a few years. And while its macho image started it out as a guy drink, because of its efficacy as an energy drink, it has evolved to serve women as well. It's the fastest-growing beverage in history.

Go into any grocery store, food mart, or gas station and you'll likely find an open bucket of Red Bull. It's a major source of profit for these stores, and has now spawned a generation of copycat beverages. More than two hundred new energy drinks arrived on store shelves in the United Kingdom during 2006, led by Red Bull, Rockstar, and Monster. We are also beginning to see a new generation of alcoholic energy drinks. Beverages like Miller's Sparks Plus and Anheuser-Busch's Tilt and Bud Extra combine caffeine and alcohol in the same beverage. Interestingly, these alcoholic energy drinks are often priced cheaper than the nonalcoholic ones. These kinds of beverages are so troubling that twenty-nine state attorneys general in August 2007 asked the Alcohol and Tobacco Tax and Trade Bureau to prevent their creators from making misleading health-related statements about them.

Research does not necessarily precede the launch of new products, and consumers—even informed consumers—don't always have a way to gauge the accuracy of the advertisements touting a product.

As head of the Public Affairs Committee of the Obesity Society (the academic society for obesity scholars in the United States, Canada, and Mexico), I found myself in the middle of a controversy about Enviga, a new beverage that was being marketed by its manufacturers, Coca-Cola and Nestlé, as "calorie burning." The launch of Enviga in trial markets occurred just before the 2006 meeting of the Obesity Society. The Public Affairs Committee responded to a poster being presented at the meeting—and an accompanying press release—that was being used to tout the new beverage. Enviga's publicity campaign suggested that the society endorsed the beverage's claim. But after reviewing the poster, our committee sent out a press release stating that Enviga had not shown any evidence that it could burn calories and reduce weight. More study was needed to substantiate the claim.

Scholars submit posters and presentations at scientific meetings; often these posters involve drug trials or studies related to food products. In this case, what seemed like a simple study of energy expenditures was in reality a very short-term study of a tiny sample. Apparently, this was all the data that Coca-Cola and Nestlé felt they needed to justify the claim that Enviga was a "calorie-burning beverage." While they didn't explicitly tout Enviga as a beverage to help you lose weight, the advertising campaign promoted it as one that burned calories, certainly implying that it would help with weight loss. And although many beverages are advertised as having some health benefit, Enviga was quite direct with its use of the term "energy burning"—without showing that it reduces weight or prevents weight gain. On February 1, 2007, the Center for Science in the Public Interest announced that it filed a lawsuit against Coca-Cola and Nestlé for making fraudulent claims. It's unclear what the ultimate result will be. More research on Enviga is under way; it might turn out to be a beverage that reduces weight. But of course, it might not reduce weight, despite the claims it has already made.

There are hundreds of other beverages on the market today—or soon to be on the market—that make what I think are at best misleading claims about their benefits. These include beverages found at cosmetic stores like Sephora. These refrigerated drinks contain mixtures of vitamins and plant extracts—they are sold as "replenishing waters" that will enhance your skin. One claims to improve skin moisture levels by 66 percent and its elasticity (its firmness) by 24 percent. If these beverages were supported by research, they would revolutionize the skin-care industry—but the research is not there. The same goes for a new class of super-beverages, including bottled water with an extra boost of oxygen; fruit juices that are being marketed as rich in antioxidants; and kombucha tea—which makes green tea seem mild in terms of its implied benefits.

3

On Movement

In times past, daily household chores, travel to and from work and school, what we did at work or school, and leisure activities ensured that we were physically active. Movement was a part of life on the farm or in the city. Surprisingly, these daily activities—both big and small—added to people's fitness and health. Continued, regular, and incremental caloric burn—from dish washing, doing laundry (the old-fashioned way), preparing food, or shopping—was significant. The same went for all the standing, lifting, and movement in our jobs. We used to walk up more stairs, we ambled about our neighborhoods to interact with friends and family, and we moved and lifted a great deal at work. With progress, our movement has changed for the worse.

In the United States, we've shifted to using the term *exercise* since there is so little movement in our daily lives unless we are engaged in leisure-time physical activity. To be sure, exercise is an important element of our overall health, but we need to think more about movement in general—not just going to a gym, but daily household and job-related tasks. The effort needed to perform day-to-day tasks has eroded over the years; some tasks have been reduced or eliminated by the introduction of technological and laborsaving devices. When we combine this lack of movement with the additional calories we consume, we get detrimental changes to our well-being.

My home in the 1950s was far different from my current home. My 1950s home had a basement, which had a concrete floor and Sheetrock walls. We washed our clothes here using a rather crude washing machine. A clothes wringer was then used to extract the water from the washed clothes, after which they were hung to dry either in the basement or outside. My mother ironed my father's shirts and pants, as well as many other items. Our basement also had a cold cellar, where we stored bags of potatoes, jars of pickles, and home-canned items for eating throughout the year.

An oil furnace provided heat for the entire house. Many of my friends' homes had a wood-burning fireplace for their primary heat. At my father's furniture store, I shoveled coal into a large burner for heat; I'd also remove all the ashes and cinders.

Our kitchen was the beating heart of our home. We had an electric oven and stove top, a refrigerator, and a small Mixmaster. We had a toaster with electric coils that turned bright red when toasting bread. It was an era, of course, without microwaves and pizza or Chinese-food deliveries. Most meals were made from scratch. After dinner, my siblings and I took turns washing the dishes. We scrubbed pots, pans, and plates by hand, rinsed and dried them, and put them away in the cabinets. Dishwashers were unheard of, and didn't become available until the early to middle 1960s.

By the mid-1950s, we had a TV set with a huge outdoor antenna. We picked up stations broadcasting from Minneapolis–St. Paul, more than one hundred fifty miles away. Our reception had a great deal of static, but we all gathered to watch our favorite programs—amounting in total to a few hours a week.

Besides biking around, I often played baseball in the backyard (using our garage door as home) or basketball in my next-door neighbors' driveway. When I was younger, I played hopscotch and hide-and-seek; as I grew older and more independent, I went to a large open field a block away, where all the boys got together year-round to play sports.

While still in elementary school, I'd borrow my father's gas lawn mower during the summer to mow lawns for other people. I had to learn to clean it, replace the spark plugs, fix the points, mix the gas and kerosene, and do all that was needed to keep it functioning. I raked the lawns before I mowed them, to remove any rocks. In winter, I shoveled snow, both at my house and for neighbors. Snowblowers and snowplows were nonexistent. You either shoveled or were homebound by the great depth of snow that blanketed northern Wisconsin.

When I compare my childhood memories with the experience of the Jones family today, I'm truly astounded by how much the world has changed. In contrast to our single television with two channels, the Joneses have four televisions (two large-screen), all wired for cable. Both Linda and Scott have televisions in their bedrooms, along with their own computers.

In the Joneses' kitchen there is a wealth of appliances, including two microwaves, a food processor, an espresso machine, and a huge double-sided refrigerator. There is a large stove with all the latest bells and whistles—griddle, induction cooktop, and warming devices. The microwave is the one appliance item they use daily. They have a gas grill, an electric garage door, a washing machine, and a dryer. Little time or energy is spent on chores compared with when I grew up.

Scott and Linda have what look to me like fancy bikes, but they never use them. They have a lot of computer games; Scott plays for hours at a time on his computer or on his Game Boy. Linda spends hours on her cell phone, in chat rooms, and text-messaging with friends. Everyone watches TV every night, and sometimes the TV remains on all day. Netflix delivers DVDs to their mailbox.

The Garcias' home is quite different. Their kitchen gadgets reflect their heritage and culinary traditions. Ana Garcia has a tortilla warmer that they use all the time. They put store-bought tortillas in it and then put the warmer into the microwave. They have a huge electric slow-cooker that they use to make bean dishes, soups, and a few other favorites. Ana has an Asian rice cooker and a simple coffeemaker. They own three TVs, one of which is always turned to Latin American soccer games. Ana, on the other hand, loves to watch American and Spanish-language soap operas. Her family calls her the Telenovela (soap opera) Queen.

The Desais' kitchen, in 1980s India, was a sharp contrast from its U.S. counterparts, past and present. Manju Desai did all her cooking on a small outside fireplace. Conditions were fairly primitive: the family had to collect wood and cow and water buffalo manure to have a fire. (Dried manure in the form of "dung patties" is a common fuel in India.) They had only a few pots, pans, and large wooden spoons to use—no other utensils or gadgets. Manju made all her chapatis (bread made from atta flour—i.e., whole-grain durum wheat, water, and salt) over the fire, and she made her own yogurt and ghee. The family owned no electrical devices—no dishwashers, televisions, or refrigerators. When I first visited that part of India, in 1965, there was no electricity in the region. But by the 1970s there was a master electricity grid in the state in which the Desais lived, though their village hadn't received access to it as of the 1980s.

The Patels—whom I visited a few years ago in northern India—had a much different kitchen. Electricity had arrived; the Patels also had a higher income and access to more modern amenities. While they also lived in a small village, Noopur had a microwave to heat the chapatis, a small refrigerator to keep her yogurt and milk (from their cow), and a propane-powered, four-burner cooktop on which to cook their meals.

Middle-class city dwellers in India live very different lives from the lives of village residents. When I visited friends in New Delhi, successful scholars who travel the world and consult with international agencies, I was surprised to see they have fewer appliances than I have in my home. But then I realized that they didn't need as many—they had a large number of servants to prepare food, clean, and do household tasks. They had a huge modern gas stove, a large refrigerator, a washer, a dryer, a microwave, and an espresso maker. (They had lived in Switzerland, where they developed a taste for strong European coffee.) But they did not have a Mixmaster or a Cuisinart. Their servants did all of the work of chopping and preparing foods.

I don't think that I or any of my friends—or that more than a few people across the globe, for that matter—would give up the time-saving devices that have freed us to live fuller, more productive lives. However, this progress comes with a cost. Somehow, we need to put back into our lives the movement—in the home, in travel, and in work—that has been eliminated by energy-saving devices.

Food preparation has changed dramatically since I was a boy. I studied food preparation in the Philippines and in the United States in the 1970s. The average woman spent about two hours a day in preparing meals. In the Philippines, we had an interviewer with a stopwatch observe how rural Filipino women and other members of the family spent their time during a three-day period in three seasons of the year. Other time-use studies elsewhere in that period put the amount of time spent in food preparation at two hours a day.

In contrast, present time-use studies indicate we use only twenty to forty minutes per day for food preparation. And this is time that is often spent simply heating up either precooked, frozen foods, or prepared foods purchased away from the home. Today, a large proportion of American families rarely cook food from scratch; in fact, many people do not know how. There has been a large decline in the amount of all kinds of housework performed by women—progress, to be sure, but again, not without a cost. We increasingly see the same pattern in high-income countries around the world. Of course, in many lower-income countries today, middle- or higher-income families have cooks and other help, as we saw with the Patels.

Looking back at the earliest documentation we have of Paleolithic man and considering the obvious lack of household technology, we can see how far we've come. As I've discussed, food preparation was a full-time occupation. For the first two million to three million years of hominid existence, food was obtained by gathering—none was produced. Our prehistoric ancestors spent all day gathering fruits, berries, a range of greens, and other vegetables. Hunting only emerged as a significant component of the subsistence pattern in the last million years. Nothing was cooked, and all transportation was by foot.

We—the human species, that is—seem to have a strong desire to discover and develop technologies that allow us to reduce our effort and thus our energy expenditure in all spheres of life. Those who could reduce their energy expenditure would be more able to survive periodic famines. In a very broad sense, you might say that evolutionary pressures have driven us to eat rich food and be lazy. And we are approaching the point where we barely have to move to flourish as a society.

Most scholars previously thought the first campfires occurred after man had a language and could communicate—about five hundred thousand years ago, as revealed by Chinese and European sites that contain hearths and burned bones. However, more recently, after decades of speculation, the anthropologist Brian Ludwig presented research on thousands of pieces of flint, showing how they had been exposed to heat to shape tools. As a result of his work, we now think that man made and used fires starting a million and a half years ago in Kenya. This does not mean that man knew how to make and control fires, or that they were as yet used for cooking, but only that they used these fires for some purpose.

Food recipes and the understanding of food or beverage preparation came much later. Eggs, shellfish, fish, and many other foods were clearly consumed long ago, but how these were actually prepared is not documented. The first use of grains—emmer and einkorn—occurred about 17,000 BCE. The history of bread and cake starts in the Neolithic period with unleavened breads. Pictures of bakers are found in early carved pictographs on tombs, and loaves of bread have been found in five-thousand-year-old Egyptian tombs. Some of these pictographs show women grinding wheat into flour, but the exact dates of the first cooked bread are not clear. Archaeologists in Egypt have also found yeast, probably used in about 4000 BCE, and many scholars have taken the presence of yeast to mean this is the time when leavened bread developed. And as noted in the previous chapter, beer originated around 10,000 BCE—the brewing of beer may be the earliest manufacturing done by man and is certainly almost as old as agriculture.

One area of speculation concerns how the origins of the wheel changed transportation and production. Data from ancient clay tablets suggest that the modern wheel did not emerge until about 3200 BCE in Mesopotamia. This seems to be when people began to expend much less effort and energy in carrying large loads of food.

Using fire for cooking was the first major culinary breakthrough. The designs of hearths and ovens and the locations of kitchens are documented in some older archaeological sites, but the evolution of methods for cooking in the past seven thousand years is not well documented. It's clear there was very slow progress in the development of cooking until the past several hundred years. Open hearths dominated for the entire earlier period and what little documentation exists indicates that peat and wood were the major sources of fuel. Coal and later oil and gas are products of a much later period; they became a common fuel option at the end of the nineteenth century. Also at the turn of the twentieth century, cooking was done on cast-iron, wood-, or coal-burning stoves. The stove, in fact, transformed cooking: kitchen walls were no longer black, and heat from the stove was used more efficiently. Of course, even in the past decade in lower income countries we continue to document respiratory infections and other problems caused by indoor use of coal- and wood-burning stoves that are poorly vented. Gas ranges became popular during the Great Depression; electric stoves came much later.

In the context of the last million years or so of human evolution, a huge number of laborsaving household devices were invented or improved upon during the twentieth century. The development of electricity laid the foundation for laborsaving technologies. It began in 1831 with Michael Faraday, who pioneered the induction of electric currents. By the end of the 1800s, electricity came to be used in the United States and elsewhere. Not only did it usher light and power into the household, but it also brought motors, stoves, irons, vacuum cleaners, washers, dryers, and dishwashers. Many major new technologies were introduced in a very short time period. Among what I consider to be major household time-saving devices, only the sewing machine came before the turn of century:

1850 *The sewing machine.* Isaac Singer invented his sewing machine and a year later formed Singer & Company.

1903 *The electric iron.*

1908 The electric *washing machine* was first mass-produced in 1908 (the exact inventor is unclear).

1909 The first *electric toaster.* At about that time, the first *vacuum cleaner* was also introduced.

1913 The first *refrigerator* and *dishwasher.* The first refrigerators for household use were developed by the General Electric Company. However, without Freon gas, which was developed in the 1930s, the earlier refrigerators (pre-1930) were dangerous.

1915 The *Mixmaster* first invented for Hobart in 1908; at this time, the KitchenAid standing mixer was introduced for the home.

1927 The Silex company introduced the first *iron with adjustable temperature control.*

1927 The first *garbage disposal* was invented.

1930s Washing machine design improved markedly during the 1930s; *spin dryers* were introduced to replace the dangerous power wringers of the day.

1935 The *Waring blender* was invented.

1947 The first *top-loading washing machine* was marketed under the Kenmore name by Sears.

1947 The first *microwave ovens* were developed, but did not become practical until the late 1960s and early 1970s.

1962 The first *iron with spray mist.*

1963 The beginning of the *self-cleaning oven.*

1972 The first *percolator with an automatic drip process* was introduced. Sunbeam develops Mr. Coffee.

1970s The first *food processor* for households was introduced by Robot Coupe.

1975 *Microwave oven* sales exceed sales of gas ranges.

In the 1960s the Desai family had none of these technologies; they cooked over a fire of wood and dung they had gathered, walked miles for their water, and even walked to a nearby river for personal toiletry needs. They didn't even have a steel grate for their wood- and dung-burning stove—they simply held pans directly over the fire. This way of existence was predominant in most of Asia, Africa, rural Latin America, and poor sections of urban Latin America until the late 1980s.

The electrification of vast areas of not only India but also much of Asia, with its population in the billions, occurred in the past twenty to thirty years. Today, access to new conveniences is skyrocketing. Since the late 1980s, my research has followed the lives of more than twenty-two thousand people in China in great detail. In 1989, only one-sixth of the families had refrigerators. Today, more than half own refrigerators and more than two-thirds own washing machines. This is a global trend. I was involved in regional development projects in the Philippines in the late 1970s and early 1980s that brought electricity into regions there. Electricity profoundly transformed the lives of these rural residents in terms of the technologies they began to use to save time and effort.

Technological change is only part of the revolution in food preparation and other household activities that previously required large amounts of time and energy. An explosion in frozen foods (introduced by Clarence Birdseye, who is credited with developing, refining, and making the quick-freezing process workable) and later in the availability of prepared meals such as TV dinners (introduced in the 1950s as Swanson's TV Dinner) has saved us tons of labor in the kitchen. The making of soup, bread, tortillas, noodles, and many other foods has been "outsourced" around the globe. Now restaurants, grocery stores, and factories provide food that only needs to be heated, or have hot water added to it—like the billions of noodle dishes con-sumed worldwide. What was at one time a repetitive, familial, and individualistic enterprise has become international and commercial.

Indoor plumbing, running water, and flushable toilets have changed the way we expend energy. These time-saving inventions accompanied the changes in the kitchen and were equally impor-tant in creating our modern lifestyle. Research conducted around the world between 1950 and 1980 revealed how much time people in rural Asia and Africa spent obtaining water and doing their toiletry. A classic study involving water in the 1960s in East Africa found that people expended about 240 calories and about forty-six minutes a day fetching water. In most of Asia and Africa, indoor running water and proximate supplies of water are changes seen only in the past twenty to thirty years; they've saved hours of walking and carrying water.

A dishwasher saves us a lot of time and requires little effort in rinsing and loading the dishes. This is nice, particularly at the end of a long day. In contrast, however, we burn 18 calories for every ten minutes we spend washing dishes by hand. When we use a washing machine, we burn only a few calories, but manual washing of clothes uses more than 2 calories each minute. When we add this up, we're burning 50 fewer calories a day compared with the way we did things a generation or two ago. For one person this is the equivalent of an extra five pounds of weight a year.

We tend to take these changes in the home for granted; but I know that many of us—on some level—are grateful that we live in a world that abounds in convenience, ease, and comfort. Of course, even in America today there are homes that don't have flush toilets or showers. But for most of us, the time we save with technology is astonishing. All told, compared with my family in the 1950s or with the families I've studied abroad, each member of the Jones family saves hundreds of calories a day in energy expenditure.

With all the time saved on household tasks, we have more time for leisure. The rub here is, however, that we're increasingly spending our leisure time on sedentary activities.

We have remote control devices for our TVs and stereos. We have cell phones and cordless phones in our homes—we no longer even have to walk to a phone. We can watch a sporting event without moving. We have our DVDs mailed to us. Our children download movies and games and then remain stationary to watch or play them. At my university, I see students sitting together and text-messaging each other; they don't bother to move a few feet to talk to each other. Similarly, movement is being taken out of our transportation. Most of us commute by car or mass transit to our workplaces. We take elevators or escalators to our offices, call for take-out lunches, and often don't even leave our desks to eat.

What do these small changes mean for obesity? An important series of studies highlighted how mechanization at home and work affects us. The shift from hand washing our clothes and dishes to using a washing machine and a dishwasher is significant. When we look at how going from using the stairs to taking an elevator or escalator has changed our lives, the effect is startling. We use about three more calories for each minute of climbing stairs than when taking an elevator or escalator. We know from other studies that we expend about 85 calories when we vacuum or dust for a half-hour and that we expend 149 calories in that same half-hour if we mop the floor.

However tiny—even trivial—these differences in calories might seem, the fact is that expending ten more calories a day equates to about a pound of weight loss a year. Washing dishes by hand each day instead of using the dishwasher would save you at least a pound or two of weight gain in a year.

In one study we undertook in China, we tracked the mode of transportation that thousands of men took to work each day—be it bicycle, motorcycle, car, bus, or walking. From 1989 to 1997, the period covered by this one study, those who rode bikes halved their likelihood of being overweight. In direct contrast, the thousands who took cars or rode motorcycles to work doubled their chances of becoming overweight.

Of course, we join gyms for aerobic exercise classes, yoga classes, or just to work out. We bike and we jog. But overall, many of these activities are expensive and hampered by hassle, safety, and other issues. (As an aside, the calorie counts given by treadmills, Stairmasters, exercise bikes, and so forth at any health club are often greatly overestimated.) Even the safety of our streets is an issue. In a national study of eighteen thousand American teenagers that we are following from high school into adulthood, we found that increased crime in the teens' neighborhoods was associated with much more time indoors watching TV and much less time outside engaging in physical activity. Traffic safety, availability of recreation options, and the financial costs of many activities are among the factors preventing young people from being as physically active.

The physical activity that we've lost at home as a result of labor-saving technology is small compared with the changes experienced at the workplace—whether at farms, factories, or service sector jobs—during the last half-century. In the 1950s, farmers burned 500 or more calories in an hour of work, but today they expend a third of that amount or less. Not only are farmers doing less work, but the proportion of Americans working in farming, mining, and forestry—the hardest jobs with the most energy expended at work—has diminished significantly. Fifty years ago, more carpenters sawed wood by hand, using 500 calories in an hour of sawing. Now, of course, they use electric saws and thus store more than half of those calories. Today, farmers and carpenters should be eating 250 fewer calories each day to account for this lost work.

The shift away from jobs in farming, mining, and forestry in industrial nations is occurring elsewhere in the world. While a larger proportion of adults work these jobs in countries with transitional economies like China and Thailand, these occupations are in rapid decline there as well. Factory work is still hard and often backbreaking, but more and more of the labor there is performed by machinery.

The service sector—jobs including secretarial work, investment banking, sales, and employment in fast-food restaurants—is rapidly growing in size. In nearly all nations more than half, if not two-thirds, of all jobs are in the service sector. And thanks to technology such as computers, copying machines, collating machines, and so on, these jobs are requiring less physical effort.

Overall, there has been a huge decline in the activity required for jobs across all sectors. Even farmers are more sedentary than ever. They can use computers to plot their plowing and fertilizing schedules, and they ride on high-tech harvesters and plows. The days of lifting bales of hay by hand, of shoveling cow manure, repairing fences, and of basic menial labor in general are over for farming in much of the higher-income world. Small family-owned nonmechanized farms in the United States have been replaced by corporate behemoths that draw on computers, satellite photos of weather and insect patterns, and sophisticated soil analysis programs that calculate how much fertilizer and water to put into each piece of land. Even in lower-income countries, tiny low-cost gas-powered hand-plows and irrigation systems are reducing what were tedious, high-calorie-burning activities such as plowing by hand and carrying buckets of water to the field.

There are still migrant laborers and others who pick fruit and other crops by hand, but increasingly mechanization is leading to reductions in energy expenditures. Farmers and other rural residents are among the most overweight populations in the United States.

In China, over the course of eleven years beginning in 1989, adults who worked at the same job—more than half in urban areas—saw their total physical activity at work reduced by half. Their likelihood of becoming overweight doubled or tripled compared with others who had the same daily calorie intake but who hadn't experienced a reduction in work energy requirements. And the millions of people around the world who have shifted from high-energy farming or manufacturing jobs into the service sector would have experienced even larger decreases in the amount of energy they expend at work.

Changes in how we travel locally are just as compelling. When I lived in India in 1965 and in China in 1989, I biked around big cities like New Delhi and Beijing. It was remarkably easy and safe. I'd never bike in these cities today; cars, buses, and pollution combine to make it far too dangerous. Today bikes are illegal in many areas of Shanghai. Cars and buses rule; there isn't room for bikers on many streets. In a few years, Shanghai will have built one of the world's largest subway systems to address congestion and pollution problems. Subways are much better for health—and for the environment. They require us to walk to and from the stations, but of course even in New York City, which has one of the most extensive subway and train systems in the world, hundreds of thousands of people still drive cars. Singapore banned cars from the core of the city to address their needs for promoting activity, controlling pollution, and saving energy. Paris has introduced a successful "rent-a-bike" initiative, and New York City's mayor, Michael Bloomberg, is trying to restrict the number of cars and trucks entering midtown Manhattan. At the time of this writing, state politics were getting in Bloomberg's way. So far he's been unsuccessful, but I hope he succeeds—we need these large changes.

The changes in our work and home lives will continue. But what's happening in our children's lives? Fewer kids walk to school; crime, traffic safety, and a litany of other concerns have led more children to be driven or taken by mass transit to school. At school today, students are spending far less time in motion than we once did. The pressure for academic success has resulted in state mandates requiring many physical education (PE) classes to be canceled or cut back. Moreover, PE classes today often include health education—a good thing—but health education versus real physical activity shouldn't be an either/or proposition.

When I was a child, each gym class began with fifteen to twenty minutes of calisthenics followed by organized games and other sports that kept us moving. Today, most children don't sweat during gym. Recess is different, too. We used to play, but today children seem to mill around outside and gossip or play with their Game Boys. The implications for our overweight and stressed-out kids (from overwork and worry) are unfortunate and significant; they don't get to work off weight or stress in exercise. For instance, in a national study we found that for eighteen thousand school children ages eleven to nineteen, less than 4 percent of their schools required daily PE. These changes aren't confined to higher-income countries but in many cases extend to schools in most lower- and middle-income countries.

In China today, few of our sample of thousands of children participate in any physical activity in school; however, with concern about the growing numbers of obese children, the government wants to mandate increases in activity across the country. But instead of a high-energy activity, the government is requiring ballroom dancing for all schools.

On Movement

In the United States, as I'll discuss in Chapter 7, there is a growing movement to increase the number of PE classes for all schools as well as to make them more rigorous. At the same time, though, some schools are banning certain sports from both gym class and recess. Especially for younger children, competitive sports are seen by many parents and educators as exclusionary and possibly hurtful to kids who aren't naturally athletic. Moreover, in most states the mandated increases aren't accompanied with more resources to hire and train teachers appropriately.

So can we increase our physical activity sufficiently to offset all the wonderful foods we eat? The answer is that, yes, we need more activity for our overall health. However, it takes a lot of exercise to work off a piece of pie. For instance, if an average piece of pecan pie contains 500 calories, it would take over two and a half hours of normal walking, almost an hour and a half of running, several hours of fast biking, or an hour of the most vigorous aerobics to offset. The same size piece of pumpkin pie would contain about 300 calories, requiring less walking—just one to one and a half hours—to burn off these calories. Also, as we get older our metabolism slows down, and so we need to expend even more energy to work off a dessert.

That two hours of work is just for dessert. Consider a cocktail, glass of wine, or bottle of beer. Two bottles of beer at twelve ounces per bottle contain at least 300 calories, requiring an hour and a half of walking to offset. If you drink half a bottle of wine at dinner, you're looking at working off 250 to 400 calories—an hour or two of walking. Personally, I love my wine. But when I drink a lot I know that I need to cut my food intake or increase my activity level considerably, or else I'll gain weight.

Think about Starbucks or any neighborhood coffee shop. A Starbucks caffelatte (venti, twenty fluid ounces) contains 340 calories—that's an hour and a half of walking. But this is nothing compared with the effort required to work off a vanilla shake at Burger King or a Baskin-Robbins medium shake, which contain 820 and 980 calories, respectively. Now you're talking about running for three or four hours.

Many of the meals at a fast-food restaurant—be it a hamburger, pizza, or taco—contain 1,000 to 2,000 calories. For instance, a meal might include a cheeseburger (500 to 750 calories), a large order of French fries (570 calories), and a large Coke (370 calories)—a total almost impossible to offset without working all day at heavy labor. A marathon runner could do this, but not an ordinary jogger.

Exercise is important. It's critical to protect the heart and to prevent a number of cancers and other diseases directly linked with low physical activity. Moreover, being fit improves our immune system and enhances our mental performance. But regardless of what we wish, we won't expend the calories we need to offset a rich dish or meal in only one day of exercise.

In terms of human evolution, we weren't built to drink Pepsi, sweetened tea and lattes, and piña coladas. So too, early humans had to work hard to survive—hunter-gatherers did a lot of walking and carrying, and humans in the last 10,000 years did a lot of making clothes, washing clothes, cleaning, and later shoeing horses, building pyramids, plowing fields, and planting crops by hand. At the end of the day, our hardworking ancestors couldn't head to the gym or to the café. But with our good fortune to be born in a better place and time comes responsibility: evolution won't cater to our appetites. We must move to offset what we eat and drink, or we will get fatter and less healthy. Modern life is no longer about unconscious movement; we have to be mindful and conscious to get it done.

4

The World Is Flat—and Fat

When I lived in India 1965 and 1966, I was completely isolated from my friends and family in the United States. It was impossible to make a phone call home. Mail service took two to three weeks for one-way mail and over a month to send a letter and receive a response. At one point, I mailed film home for my parents to have developed. I didn't know that my camera lens had a problem; it took me two months to learn that many rolls of pictures I took in my travels around India were ruined. There was no TV, and I had access to Indian newspapers only.

When I travel to India, China, or anywhere else in the world today it is a very different experience. I can watch CNN at my hotel, use a cell phone to call home, check my e-mail, and order almost any major U.S. newspaper—downloaded and then printed at the hotel. At just about any time I can communicate with anyone, anywhere. I'm completely in touch with my students, colleagues, friends, my son, and the rest of my family.

This shift in communications capability is just one element of a transition that has been going on for thousands of years, but that has greatly accelerated in the past several decades.

During my first visit to India, I couldn't buy everything I needed in the way of toiletries or food. If I wanted something that would remind me of home, a bottle of Coke was my one option. It was impossible to buy American toothpaste, for example. When I return to Delhi or Beijing today, I can stop at Wal-Mart and other Western-style super-stores. When my son lived in Beijing for his junior year abroad during college in 2004 and 2005, he lived just a few blocks from a Carrefour, a French version of Wal-Mart. He could buy anything there.

Just as new technology has changed information flow, it has transformed the entire chain of events from food production to consumption. I can buy almost anything in the United States that I can buy overseas. Food, clothing, and many luxury items are available in most midsize and large cities in this country, and on the Web. I might not be able to find perfectly ripened cheese as in France, or such good bread and pastries, or even the same local, inexpensive wines, but in terms of processed, packaged food the access is pretty much there. And sometimes the converse is true—I can buy wines or clothing items that aren't available in their country of origin.

In general, all this has changed more gradually in the United States than in Asia, Latin America, the Middle East, and Africa. In Russia, where I have gone annually since 1991, the changes in what I can buy are striking. When I first started working in the former Soviet Union, the money I had was in U.S. dollars. I was allowed to go to a special store for those with U.S. dollars to buy goods that were unavailable in Moscow, such as Crest toothpaste, chewing gum, or dark chocolate bars from Switzerland and France. When I worked in Kyrgyzstan it was worse—there was almost no food available unless I went to a similar store that accepted only dollars. But only a few years later I could buy those same items on the streets of Moscow at hundreds of little kiosks. In the following years, large supermarkets in Moscow began to carry the same foods and beverages that we buy in the United States and Western Europe.

As I've already discussed, across the globe we've seen a virtual revolution in what we drink. There was no bottled water—or any other beverages besides Coke—in India in the 1960s. Today, store shelves are heavily stocked. But we've also seen big changes in what is available in the United States—each year the beverages we drink change significantly. The newest fad beverage is as likely to come from Austria—as Red Bull did a few years ago—or from Eastern Europe as it is to come from the U.S. beverage giants.

As Thomas Friedman wrote in his 2005 book *The World Is Flat*, "The economic and political systems all opened up during the course of the 1990s so that people were increasingly free to join the free market game." He was speaking of the people of China, India, Russia, Eastern Europe, and Central Asia joining the global economy.

But this isn't just something that has happened from 1990 on. Interaction among people around the world has been going on—albeit on a much smaller scale—for hundreds of years, especially where food is concerned. Coffee was introduced to India from Ethiopia by way of Arab traders. It subsequently reached Latin America, where the genetic stock of the coffee traces back to a coffee plant from Java via a botanical garden in Amsterdam. Spain and the Middle East didn't have citrus fruit until it came from India during the fourteenth or fifteenth century. Islamic traders shipped fruits to Persia and later via North Africa to Spain.

Similarly, the first documentation of any kind of noodles is a pot of thin yellow noodles that was preserved for four thousand years in the silt of the Yellow River in China. This find ended any suggestion that the Italians or Arabs first developed the noodle. It is popularly believed that Marco Polo introduced Chinese noodles to Italy in the thirteenth century, and that ravioli is a derivative of the Chinese wonton. But durum wheat pasta seems to have existed since Roman times and to have come to Italy from China much earlier than Marco Polo's time, though the exact dates are unclear.

These are just small examples of a process that really began when we stopped being nomadic and entered the agricultural period. Trading, migration, religion, conquest, and other major transitions spread our customs, flora, fauna, and food around the globe. As far as food goes, global trade is not new. Globalization has been going on for a long time; however, it was exceedingly slow until the recent period.

The increasingly rapid changes in connectivity, integration, and interdependence in all spheres of life—technological, cultural, economic, and social—that we've seen in the last couple of decades obviously have significant effects on our everyday lives, including how much we weigh. The freer movement of capital, technology, goods, and services has profoundly affected both our diet and activity, and has created subsequent imbalances that have led to the obesity epidemic.

The new accessibility to supermarkets in many places across the globe is a cornerstone of change in the food system. A second change is the increased availability of low-cost vegetable oils to the developing world. As a result of this, lower-income countries can now consume fat levels equivalent to those of higher-income countries. A third change springs from the transformation of the major staples in many countries, such as changes to the production and consumption of the tortilla in Mexico.

The foremost broad-based change in the global food system is occurring in food distribution. We don't know exactly how the introduction of the Wal-Marts, Carrefours, Aholds, and other global supermarkets is affecting our dietary intake patterns, but we are sure that the changes are mixed—some good and some bad.

In the United States, changes in food distribution have been gradual. Before supermarkets, grocers picked out food items for their patrons—that is, there was no self-service; most food products were stored out of the shopper's reach in bins and jars. The first supermarket chain began in the 1910s with the Piggly Wiggly in Tennessee. Soon other small chains emerged, all following the Piggly Wiggly model of self-service. That began a period in which we moved from bulk storage of foods to individual packaging. Sanitation improved as did quality control. Slowly, grocery store chains such as Safeway, Kroger, and Giant emerged and, between 1930 and 1950, became the self-service packaged goods purveyors that we know today. These stores increased in size until we saw Wal-Mart and others like it revolutionize size, pricing, labor, and other practices. Studies show that Wal-Mart's entry into any geographic area, be it in the United States or abroad, results in food prices of 15 percent lower or more at both Wal-Mart and ultimately in the community as a whole.

In the developing world the changes have been more rapid, and are more profound. The fresh markets that we think of as farmers' markets (and which people in trade circles often call "wet markets") are disappearing as the major source of food. So are small markets and tiny stores that sell just a few products. They are being replaced by large supermarkets—usually part of larger multinational chains like Carrefour or Wal-Mart, or in countries such as South Africa and China, by local chains that mimic Wal-Mart. China has both global and local chains, whereas a smaller country like South Africa has its own domestically grown chain that is expanding across the urban areas of sub-Saharan Africa. These chains function in similar ways—they cut costs, improve efficiencies, and become a major purchaser that can bargain with suppliers for lower prices and other economies of scale.

In Latin America, the supermarkets' share of all retail food sales increased from 15 percent in 1990 to 60 percent by 2000. For comparison, 80 percent of retail food sales in the United States in 2000 occurred in supermarkets. The expansion of supermarkets in Latin America in one decade is equivalent to about a half-century of expansion in the United States. Supermarkets have spread across both large and small countries, from capital cities to rural villages, and from use by upper- and middle-class families to use by working-class families. This global expansion is in different stages and occurring at varying rates across Asia, Eastern Europe, and Africa.

In India, the bulk of retail outlets are still neighborhood shops. Carrefour, Wal-Mart, and others are spending billions to break into this market. From various reports, the Indian mass-retailer market appears to be growing by at least $27 billion per year—which is bigger than the gross domestic product of half of the countries of the world. India's growing middle class wants these changes, wants to shop more easily in air-conditioned comfort, and wants the benefits of choice and variety that the global food conglomerates offer. There are a lot of factors behind the rise of supermarkets. Consumer demand for processed and safer foods is on the rise in developing countries. As countries modernize, women earn more and are more likely to want to work outside the home—creating a demand for prepared foods, which save time. Transportation and access to technology, such as refrigerators, has played a role in the demand for, and access to, supermarkets. Furthermore, improvements in the logistics and procurement systems used by the supermarkets have allowed them to compete in terms of cost with the more typical outlets in developing countries—the small mom-and-pop stores and open public markets—for fruits, vegetables, and other products.

Supermarkets are large providers of processed, higher-fat, added-sugar, and salt-laden foods in developing countries, but they have also been the purveyors of some good. For example, supermarkets were instrumental in the development of the ultra-high temperature (UHT) process that gives milk a long shelf life and provides a safe source of milk for all income groups. Supermarkets are also key players in establishing food safety standards. Most important, they have solved the problems of what is called the "cold chain"—namely, ways to get perishable milk, fruits and vegetables, and meats safely to the consumer. In many instances, mega-markets have brought higher-quality produce to urban residents year-round—consumers in many countries can obtain fresh fruits and vegetables throughout the year as opposed to the seasonality of local farmers' markets.

We might take these benefits of seasonal availability as a given in higher-income countries. For instance, in the United States we can get plums, tomatoes, or berries in the winter from South America and in the summer from our own local markets. However, this is a major shift for most lower- and middle-income countries.

It remains to be understood how these mega-supermarkets will affect the contents of our diet and how much we eat in total. There has been only one study on this topic, which took place in 2000 in Guatemala. Perhaps not surprisingly, this study suggests that supermarkets are linked with increased purchases of processed food items, including pastries, cookies, sweets, chocolate, and ice cream at the expense of more basic foodstuffs such as corn and beans. We need research that reveals how these new food markets affect overall prices as well as relative prices of different food group categories. For instance, if candy and baked goods become less expensive relative to fruits and vegetables, it is obviously not good for nutrition. But it would be a good thing if soft drinks and candy became more expensive than milk and fruit. We need to determine how the mega-markets affect our consumption of refined versus complex carbo-hydrates, calorically sweetened foods, animal-source foods, fruits, and vegetables—among other important matters.

Around the world, there has also been a big change in the fats used for cooking and food processing. The edible vegetable oils story is particularly important, as its effects have been profound.

Until the decade following World War II, most fats available for human consumption were animal fats such as milk, butter, and meat—except in the Mediterranean world, where olive oil is omni-present. But then a revolution in the production and processing of oilseed-based fats occurred. Today, the principal vegetable oils are soy-bean, sunflower, rapeseed, palm, and peanut oil. Technological break-throughs in the development of high-yield oilseeds and in the refining of high-quality vegetable oils greatly reduced the cost of baking and frying fats, margarine, butterlike spreads, salad oils, and cooking oils in relation to animal-based products. In addition, worldwide demand for vegetable fats was fueled by health concerns after studies showed that the consumption of animal fats had negative effects on choles-terol. Furthermore, a number of significant economic and political ini-tiatives led to the development of oil crops, not only in Europe and the United States, but also in Southeast Asia (palm oils), in Brazil, and in Argentina (soybean oils). As a result of all this, from 1945 to 1965 there was almost a fourfold increase in the U.S. production of vegeta-ble oils, while animal fat production increased by only 11 percent.

The shift toward a higher-fat diet in developing nations began with increases in the domestic production and imports of edible oils, rather than increased imports of meat and milk. With the excep-tion of peanut oil, global availability of vegetable oils approximately tripled from 1961 to 1990. Soybeans provide the largest proportion of vegetable oil consumed worldwide. Many of these processed oils are not well regulated, and some of the newer oils are highly pathogenic. For instance, Walter Willett and Indian scholars have shown that many of the vegetable oils sold in India consist of over 50 percent trans-fatty acids. In oil sold in China, we found a large amount of the potentially pathogenic myristic acid.

At the moment, prices of edible oils are rising as a result of the increasing use of corn and other oilseeds for biodegradable fuel. According to research by colleagues at the International Food Policy Research Institute in Washington, D.C., demand resulting from biofuels increased the price of corn and other energy crops by an estimated 33 percent in early 2008. This may be a short-term price increase—supplies will likely grow in response to the rising prices of the past two years. If supplies don't grow, however, the higher price of vegetable oil will affect the cost of baked and fried foods. The effects of this on consumption are unclear, but one thing is for sure—the long-term trend of the growing availability of vegetable oils has led to a big increase in the amount of fat in the global diet.

For Mexicans, for thousands of years, a table without tortillas was an empty table. The tortilla is the centerpiece of the meal—the food that for centuries has been the soul of their cuisine. Pre-Hispanic peasants in Mexico developed a labor-intensive approach to creating tortillas. They used a utensil called the *metate*, a tablet of black volcanic rock that sat on three stubby legs and sloped forward and downward. The *metate* was used to grind corn for tortillas and tamales. It was also used to grind chilies, seeds, coffee, and other items. Until the turn of the twentieth century, and even later, women would spend four to five hours a day preparing tortillas to feed their families. The work would begin the night before, when the corn was simmered with lime and water, a process known as nixtamalization. After boiling, the mixture was left to soak overnight, ground in the morning to make a moist dough, and then cooked over a fire on an earthenware griddle. The dough did not keep nor did the tortillas last beyond the day they were made, as they became hard. In contrast, the nixtamalized corn does keep for a couple of days. There was a real art to tortilla making; women who made them well gained status, and women even needed to be able to make them to get married.

Commercial mills were started in the 1920s. Women flocked to them. The corn was still prepared by the traditional water and lime process and the tortillas were cooked in the home, but women saved time by paying a small amount to have the corn ground. Then, dehydrated corn flour was developed. This change was so gradual that today's tortilla, while unrecognizable compared with the tortilla of 1900, was accepted by consumers as tastes and preferences adapted to each gradual step in the tortilla's evolution. Eventually, the entire process was outsourced, starting in the postwar period with the development of small factories that ground the corn, which later integrated dough-making and the forming and cooking of the tortillas. It took a long time, but by the 1950s these factories existed everywhere in urban Mexico and gradually began to appear in rural areas as well. They were still small in scale.

Peasants whom I have visited, still living in isolated communities like those in Chiapas, continued to make their own tortillas well into the late 1990s, but this is changing. When I visited Chedraui, a Mexican version of Wal-Mart, in the summer of 2007 in Chiapas, there was a line of customers in front of the tortilla-making machine. They were waiting for their freshly made tortillas to take home for the family.

Moreover, the corn itself has changed. In the early 1990s, the Mexican subsidy to corn millers was cut as the government tried to focus its resources on assistance directly targeted to the poor. So, by the new millennium, the government was providing money and food to the poor and malnourished instead of subsidizing corn. Just as the subsidies were eliminated, cheap corn came to Mexico from the United States. The North American Free Trade Agreement (NAFTA) made that possible. The cheap, subsidized yellow corn from the United States drove many Mexican farmers out of the corn market. While Mexicans haven't liked the changes in taste that result from using the U.S. corn, they do accept them. Did NAFTA cause these problems and changes? Or are the changes we find today the result of a long chain of events that on the one hand liberated rural and poor urban women and on the other hand changed the cuisine and the healthfulness of the tortillas themselves? I'd argue that NAFTA accelerated changes whose roots go back many years.

There are subtle but important nutritional effects resulting from this process of modernization. The classic corn tortilla was consumed with beans. A traditional Aztec and Mayan cropping pattern was to plant the corn interspersed with beans, which enriched the soil and prevented erosion. Their cuisine, refined over many centuries, produced a balanced, healthful diet that also provided complete protein. As manufactured corn tortillas replaced homemade ones, corn production and corn and bean planting combinations were replaced. The Mexican diet, particularly among the low-income population, is still corn-based, but today's tortilla is not as healthy. The Mexican government now sees the need to fortify corn flour for tortillas as a means of providing micronutrients that are deficient in the current diet.

The decrease in corn farming is just one of the many ways that global economics have affected the activity patterns and diets of Mexicans. And of course, the people of most countries—if not all—are experiencing lifestyle changes as a result of globalization. Staples like chapatis in India and rice and noodles in China and Southeast Asia are changing as rapidly as are tortillas. Go to any Asian country and you'll see instant noodles all over the place. They've replaced hundreds of possibly healthier, less refined noodles consumed across the region. The traditional Indian chapati is made with one of the healthiest varieties of whole wheat, whole-grain durum wheat. But when I was in India in November 2007, I was surprised to see how many Indians had shifted from whole wheat or coarse grain-based traditional breads to bread made with refined, bleached flour.

One of the least discussed and least understood areas of change affecting dietary and physical activity patterns is the role of the mass media. Throughout the developing world, there has been a profound increase in the ownership of television sets and the penetration of modern, Western-oriented television programming and advertising. This has been accompanied by a proliferation of magazines and access to DVDs of Western movies. The Internet and cell phones add to this increased access to advertising as well as to ideas about the diets and lives of people in other cultures. It's unclear how all this affects how we eat, drink, and move. Many accuse TV of being directly responsible for child obesity—it encourages sedentary activity and allows for the direct marketing of fried and sugary food to children.

Television ownership is a recent phenomenon in China. In 1989, almost 63 percent of households owned a TV, with 49 percent of sets being black and white. By 2000, more than 91 percent of Chinese households owned a TV, 68 percent of which were color sets.

While the majority of American children watched more than five hours of television a day in the late 1990s, the average Chinese child spent about an hour a day watching TV and/or playing video games. Only about 10 percent watched TV for more than one hour a day and fewer than 5 percent played video games for more than one hour a day. The difference is one of family pressures. In China, children study and are sedentary, whereas in the United States, children do not study as much, but in their nonstudy time parents don't tend to restrict their TV and video game time. Now, however, Chinese children are watching more TV.

Earlier Chinese TV came from either a provincial or a national set of channels. The first Chinese television advertisements appeared on a Shanghai channel in 1979. Even as late as the 1990s only a few million Chinese saw advertising on TV. But by 2006 this changed drastically. Now, with the increasing availability of cable and satellite TV beamed from Hong Kong—such as Phoenix TV (often called Hong Kong Star), a Rupert Murdoch–owned network similar to Fox in the United States—they have access to many of the shows that we see in the West, which are usually dubbed into Mandarin. Of course, along with the shows, they see advertisements for junk food products just like in North America and Europe. Today, China is considered the world's fastest-growing TV advertising market.

Similar increases in television ownership and viewership are happening in all regions of the developing world. There has yet to be serious research on how these rapid changes in media have affected attitudes, knowledge, and behavior related to how the billions of people in these emerging markets eat, drink, and move. I think that when these studies are done, the results will show that large shifts in attitudes toward food and eating behavior are linked with modern TV viewing and increased advertising.

Many blame "Coca-Colonization," or the spread of fast foods around the world, as a key culprit in the worldwide surge in obesity. Some researchers think that the spread of the U.S. fast-food and soft drink industries has led to the decline of healthy traditional local cuisines throughout the developing world. Today, Coca-Cola is sold in more than two hundred countries. More than half of McDonald's sales are made outside the United States. Besides McDonald's, Pizza Hut and KFC are rapidly spreading around the globe. They are quickly followed by—or even preceded by—local food chains that follow their models, even to the point of serving the same dishes.

Do these thousands of McDonald's and KFC outlets indeed change the way the world eats? Are they leading people away from their healthy traditional diets to higher-fat, sugar-laden, prepared-away-from-home food products? Are they leading to increased portion sizes worldwide, as they have in the United States? The answer depends on which country you study and how you examine the data.

I participated in research on children's food intake in four large countries—the Philippines, Russia, China, and the United States. We discovered that kids in the Philippines ate and snacked away from home as much as children in the United States. This wasn't true for China and Russia. In those two countries, few children drank soft drinks or ate fast food. American and Filipino youth consumed more than a third of their daily calories from foods prepared away from home—either eaten in restaurants or fast-food establishments in the United States or brought home from small cafeterias and street vendors, as in the Philippine city of Cebu.

In contrast, Chinese children consumed very little of their total energy from foods prepared or eaten outside of the home, except for snack foods (typically a biscuit, some peanuts, or fruit). Eating in restaurants is rare among Chinese families, and there isn't yet a tradition of bringing prepared foods into the home, nor is there a prevalent practice of taking children out to restaurants. Thus, our studies show that while some differences in children eating fast food might relate to the accessibility of fast-food outlets, much of the difference is a result of custom. Locally prepared snack foods and stalls and restaurants have always existed in China and Russia, but families in these societies don't have the same tradition of eating so much food away from home.

Anthropologists who have tried to understand the impact of McDonald's from the consumer's perspective find a complex picture. Despite widespread criticism of McDonald's as a symbol of foisting on other people a diet just like ours in the United States, studies show that not all of the changes attributed to McDonald's presence overseas have been negative. These scholars found that in Hong Kong and China, for instance, the McDonald's staff were friendly and courteous, and prided themselves on providing a very clean restaurant, eating area, and restrooms.

McDonald's has also been forced to adapt to local culture and tastes. In China, for example, Chicken McNuggets come with the traditional sauces and also a chili-garlic sauce. Crispy chicken wings are also a menu item. In India, to cater to religious sensitivities, beef and pork products aren't served. Chicken, which is prepared according to Islamic law, along with fish, is the only meat product used. There are separate areas for vegetarian and meat dishes. The Chicken McGrill sandwich is a thin chicken patty served with thin slices of both onions and tomatoes, and with green chutney replacing the usual layer of mayonnaise. Also very popular is the vegetarian burger, which includes a vegetable patty (made of potato, peas, and spices), tomato, onion, and an eggless mayonnaise. McDonald's has undergone a complex process of cultural accommodation, compromise, and change in its assimilation into Asian societies.

It isn't possible to link changes in fast-food intake in these countries with increases in obesity. However, the shift toward on-the-go eating as opposed to the slower eating of the past is a profound change. The lack of conclusive research on how Western or local fast-food chains are affecting the quantity and quality of food and the overall weight gain is a sharp contrast to the very large number of studies on this topic in the United States. It's virtually impossible to place blame on any one source of food or beverage for increases in obesity across the globe. Nor is that the right approach. For example, I think that Coke and Pepsi play a huge role in obesity in Mexico, but their role in many other countries such as China is trivial. And I don't think we have the clear evidence yet to exactly state the role of the fast-food companies. At the same time, we do know they play a key role, and we do need them to change (as I discuss in Chapter 6).

As we've seen, globalization has been part of our history for centuries. But it has a new engine that is accelerating it. In January 1995, after eight years of negotiations, the General Agreement on Tariffs and Trade (GATT) was replaced by a stronger organization—the World Trade Organization (WTO). Today, there are 148 WTO member countries, and WTO rules apply to more than 98 percent of international trade. The WTO has increasingly expanded the scope of its work from its original narrow focus on reducing tariffs on manufactured goods to eliminating barriers in all sectors in favor of a "free trade" agenda. Unlike most international agreements, there are financial penalties and sanctions that the WTO uses to enforce its rules. This gives the WTO greater power to propel and promote the increase of trade in services, commodities, processed products, technology, and investments.

Certainly the example of the tortilla in Mexico and the role of NAFTA in allowing subsidized American corn to be sold in Mexico reveals the power of global trade.

Another example can be found in South Korea, where international fast-food chains have used the new WTO rules to enter what was a restricted market. Previously, South Korea had purposely focused on its traditional diet as one of the ways to keep its population healthy. The centerpieces of traditional Korean cuisine are rice and a large number of vegetable dishes. Typically for lunch and dinner there were five to ten servings of mushrooms, sweet potatoes, cucumbers, varieties of kimchi (spicy fermented cabbage), lettuce, and other greens that were used as wrappings instead of bread. This diet had little meat and a very low fat content. It nourished a population that was unusually thin for its high level of income and its access to technology and all things modern. In fact, the proportion of fat in the diet and the number of obese South Koreans was one-third or less than what might have been expected for the nation's income level. When their country joined the WTO in 1995, however, by law South Koreans couldn't stop global food and restaurant chains from moving in. Given its high per capita income, South Korea was a prime market for Western food and restaurant companies. In 2007, for example, the per capita GNP of South Korea was $25,000, making it the eleventh most wealthy nation in the world. Analyses of initial, anecdotal, and descriptive information about the thirteen years since South Korea entered the WTO show a marked shift in the composition of the population's diet and the obesity patterns across the country. Obesity is rising quickly, vegetable intake is going down, and a rapid Westernization of one of the globe's healthiest cuisines appears to be under way.

It's easy to blame globalization for all of the evil in the developing world. However, as I've noted, many of the changes are what we'd expect to see with improved incomes and access to better and more varied food. And many changes began centuries or even thousands of years ago. No one wants to eat a monotonous diet of rice, beans, corn, and vegetables—with a little fish—if a tastier diet is available. Similarly, no one wants to do the heavy backbreaking labor of the past. Having spent some time on a rice farm in the Philippines some time ago, I can say that it's not pleasant—I never want to do again the work of transplanting, weeding, and the other labor-intensive tasks required. Small hand-driven plows for spreading fertilizer and newer technologies for threshing and grinding rice are major improvements in the quality of life for these farmers.

The same is true for the efforts involved in pulling a rickshaw or carrying hundreds of pounds around a dock, warehouse, or factory in Asia decades ago, even though the thousands of calories burned by such work helped keep weight off. Again, eliminating this work by the use of equipment is a major improvement in the quality of life.

Edible oil makes food tastier. People in Asia and Africa love these oils—and use them a lot. We cannot deny that sugar also makes food taste better.

Modern television and Internet access also makes life more interesting. They open us up to understanding each other—for better and for worse.

We can benefit or be hurt by any of these changes, but they are desired by almost everyone. The mystery is not how to stop development and modernization, but how to adjust our way of living, eating, and drinking so that we can gain from these changes—not be destroyed by them. We need to look to industry, government, our communities, and individuals to make these changes work for us.

5

The Big Problems
of a Fat World

Upon graduating from college in the 1960s, I entered the world as one of those youths focused on ending all injustices. When I lived in India in 1965 and 1966, I witnessed great poverty in the slum areas of Old Delhi and in villages in the north. I saw hunger, starvation, and unemployment everywhere. When I lived and worked in urban slums and poor areas of the northern United States from 1969 to 1971, I saw a different kind of poverty—but real, just the same. Hunger was a common theme in both countries, though its consequences were much harsher in India because it killed so many children, many of them not yet even preschoolers.

While in the squatter areas of India, I went from house to house interviewing and visiting families. I lived with friends in their villages. I return often, and the fact that I speak Hindi allows me to enter worlds not open to most Westerners. Indian families are particularly open to sharing with foreigners who show a strong interest in their world. During 1965, I lived in a *jhuggi-jhopri,* that very densely populated squatters' area, in Old Delhi near the Jumna River

Bridge and close to where there are now memorial ghats for Nehru. The huts were one story high and made of tin, cardboard, wood, and whatever materials their residents could find. They had tiny fires for cooking and no protection from the winter cold. The population density is almost impossible for an American to understand—more than two hundred thousand people per square mile. If I got sick the people would do anything they could for me. They always offered me tea that was boiled and sanitized. I knew, however, this represented about one-third of their daily income, so I always turned it down for water unsuitable for drinking. As a result, I had frequent gastrointestinal problems and returned to the United States looking emaciated and weak. (When I arrived on the West Coast and was met by an uncle, he was shocked. I learned later that he called my parents and said I looked "like Gandhi" and that he would try to feed me and get me back to normal.)

Living daily amid the poverty, I met malnourished men, women, and children, but I didn't understand their conditions as well as I do now. At least once a month I encountered a family in which a child had died. Although the people looked quite thin—many did not look healthy—they had a vibrant life filled with music, humor, and much love. I learned to look beyond the squalor and hunger to this other, brighter side and in doing so—of course—I was protecting myself from the immense underlying misery and stress.

When I first visited the Desai family during the 1980s in their village in the northern state of Uttar Pradesh, I didn't feel that they were any richer or poorer than the people I met in the urban squatter areas in the 1960s. The adults and their four children were all very thin; three of the children had been particularly tiny at birth. The Desais also had two children who had died—one during childbirth and one at about eight months. The first child died probably of low birth weight. The second died during the weaning period, when breast milk was no longer adequate; the children were exposed to many environmental contaminants, and their diet of gruel—made of grains and water—was of poor nutritional quality.

My experiences were typical of life in India. There were few overweight people—just a few wealthy landowners—in either the urban or rural areas. Women showed their midriffs when dressed in their saris; I rarely saw rings of fat on their bellies, except when I attended the wedding of a very wealthy person.

When I returned to India in 2006, I visited the Patel family. Times had changed. This family of five also lived in a rural area, but they were quite well off. Gopal and Noopur Patel both had rather large bellies—Noopur's hung out of her sari. I could see that the older son, who was twelve, was also overweight and was rapidly moving toward being obese. Frankly, I expected to see some of this when I visited India. Having worked in China since 1987, I've witnessed how the proportion of overweight Chinese has exploded from a few percent to over one-third of all adults.

But India and China, in this respect, pale in comparison with Mexico. Mexicans living in Mexico seem to eat and live no differently from how the Garcias live in the United States, and they're equally overweight. In Mexico, we've seen changes in diet in the last decade that are similar to those experienced by the Garcia family since they moved to the United States. The Garcia family emigrated from the Chiapas region of Mexico in 1985 to a Los Angeles suburb. They moved during a time when Mexicans, in particular the rural Mayans, were still experiencing a great deal of hunger and malnutrition. Today, however, all of the Garcias are heavy; both parents and several of the children are obese. Cesar (the father) has been diagnosed with the Mexican disease of *"azucar en la orina,"* or "sugar in the urine"—adult-onset type 2 diabetes. It's revealing that Mexicans have such a popular term to describe diabetes. In the United States we tend to acknowledge that we have diabetes when the doctors diagnose us. In Mexico, when people begin to suffer from the symptoms linked with diabetes, such as frequent urination, increased fatigue, and excessive thirst, they start to tell friends and family, "I have sugar in my urine"—"*azucar en la orina.*" I won't be surprised if Cesar quickly develops eye problems (such as glaucoma), kidney problems, and other complications related to his diabetes. Without medical insurance, he has no way to pay for the device he needs to monitor his blood sugar, which costs one hundred dollars, or for the expensive medication required to control his condition.

Compounding the problem are Cesar's beliefs about how he got diabetes and the way he and his family are addressing the need to alter his diet and lose weight as requested by his doctor during the one medical visit he was able to make. Cesar thinks that some type of scare or shock—he used the word *susto*—occurred one day. His belief, very much based on folklore and a Mexican tradition, is that he was drinking water and this water in combination with the *susto* is what gave him the diabetes.

Cesar's doctor has told him to stop eating certain foods, such as Mexican sweet rolls, and to stop drinking soft drinks to cut his sugar intake. His doctor also told him to cut down his overall eating—particularly to curb his newfound interest in pizza—and to reduce his weight. But his family and relatives weren't very supportive. They've said this will not help: it was the *susto*—not his diet or lifestyle—that caused the problem. They also feel that the needs of his family and friends should come before his need to control his diabetes—needs that relate to the family's love of sugar and high-fat fried foods. Cesar's doctor clearly didn't understand the cultural background shaping the family's response to his patient's condition. Nor did he have the ability to get help for him in the way of a health educator who could work with the entire family on this issue and help teach Cesar how to control this disease.

Also, the youngest Garcia child and the older girl are extremely overweight for their ages. Felix weighs sixty-one pounds and is four feet tall. Maria is five feet tall and weighs 147 pounds. Maria has also begun to complain about being super thirsty; the parents plan to consult with friends to decide if they should send her to a doctor.

It's a frustrating situation, but not one limited to the Garcias. We may not often see the same folklore in the United States, but we do find that a large proportion of our population—not only Hispanics but also many other American residents, white and black—aren't able to overcome family resistance to change or are simply unable to try to make changes in diet and activity themselves. In other words, a large proportion of U.S. residents poorly control their diabetes. Studies indicate that blacks and Hispanics more often than whites will not adhere to their medication regime and will thus suffer many more complications of diabetes. Of course, this is most likely a result of income and education rather than race, but, as we've seen, there is an added element of cultural differences that is difficult to overcome.

In Mexico, where I've been working quite a bit in the last few years, less than one-third of all adults were overweight or obese in 1988. But in 2006, 71 percent of women and 65 percent of men were overweight or obese. More startling is that there were almost no obesity-related diseases like diabetes in 1988, but today diabetes is that nation's new scourge—it's as common as malnutrition was twenty years ago. Pediatric overweight is also rapidly increasing. Currently, about one-quarter of Mexican children are overweight or obese, but I anticipate that these levels will increase to far beyond that. While there is some government care available for diabetics, Mexico doesn't have the resources to properly treat all individuals with diabetes. Monitoring and expensive drug treatment are needed, and so is education to teach people not only how to control their disease, but—more important—how to prevent it.

When I think about the changes that have taken place in the United States, I recall that when I was growing up in Superior, Wisconsin, my brother was the only child in my age range who had the slightest concern about his weight. (I'm sure, however, that there were others.) At school, there were few children in any class who were very heavy. We didn't ostracize anyone. Weight was of no consequence to my friends or me. I was aware that some of my parents' friends were heavy, but they moved well, seemed healthy, and in no way were debilitated by their weight. During the 1960s, my political work as a civil rights activist and a summer of working for the U.S. poverty program (through the Office of Economic Opportunity) took me to the coal country of West Virginia, to the rural South, and later to the urban ghettos of the North. I remember seeing heavy people—some of the black women as well as a lot of white men. Some of the black ministers and activists with whom I worked were also very heavy, but I wasn't all that conscious of this issue then; our focus was, ironically, on hunger. In fact, eradicating hunger in America was a major effort at that time. There were national hearings on poverty in Appalachia. Throughout the South there was a lot of publicity about displaced poor sharecroppers and the rural poor. Our goal was to get subsidized food programs into all of the schools that lower-income children attended and to provide food stamps for the poor so they could eat adequately.

In contrast, when I spent time with the Jones family in 2006, conditions had obviously changed. The whole family had a weight problem. Bob Jones, who was in his early forties and worked at an insurance company, had developed a serious weight problem and had hypertension. He had slowly added weight over the twenty years of his marriage. Ellen Jones, a schoolteacher, and fifteen-year-old Linda were also quite heavy, while nine-year-old Scott was plump, though still short and yet to have his growth spurt. Often when they reach puberty, heretofore pudgy boys become lean and muscular as their rate of growth finally outpaces their rate of weight gain. Ideally, their bodies balance around this time.

Of course, the Patels, Garcias, and Joneses provide only a glimpse of the world we're living in today. In more than eighteen countries, over half the population is overweight or obese. In six countries (the rich ones being the United States, England, and Australia and the poor ones being Egypt, Mexico, and South Africa) two-thirds of adults are overweight or obese. And these six countries are only the tip of the global obesity pyramid. The world is fat.

The map on page 108 provides some sense of the proportion of countries in which more than half the population is overweight. For the countries in white, I don't have nationally representative data. North America, Russia and Eastern Europe, much of Latin America and South America, the Middle East, and Australia stand out for having over half of their adult populations overweight or obese.

My research, as well as that of colleagues from Brazil, has shown increasing rates of overweight and obesity among adults across the world. In a few countries, we have adequate data to show that rates of change are accelerating. The percentage of both adults and children in the United States who become overweight and obese each year has increased since the decades before 1994. (The rate of increase for children is not as great as the rate for adults, but nonetheless is very high.) About 0.5 percent of the children in most countries are becoming overweight each year. For example, in 2006 there were about 1.8 billion children in the moderate- and low-income countries of the world (a figure that is likely on the low side). So this means that about nine million children in these poorer countries would become overweight over the course of a year. And of the approximately three billion adults in these same countries, 1 percent become overweight each year. This is equivalent to approximately thirty million new

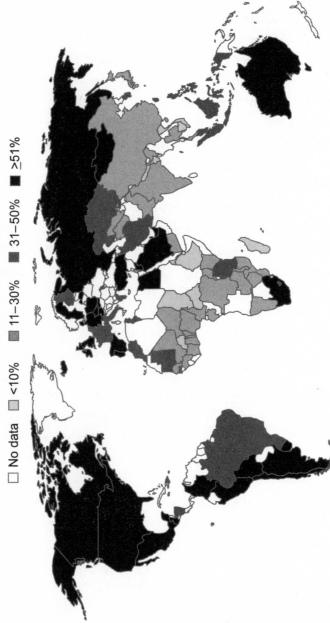

Global Overweight and Obesity
Percent of Adult Population

☐ No data ■ <10% ■ 11–30% ■ 31–50% ■ ≥51%

(Body Mass Index > 25. Based on nationally representative samples, ages 20 to 49.)

overweight adults each year. (The numbers for adults and children are both rough figures.)

In higher-income countries, we have evidence that the increases in overweight have been occurring for much of the century. One of the most useful studies looked at children in Denmark from 1930 to 1983. The study reviewed the Copenhagen municipal school records, in which weight and other measurements were recorded on an annual basis for children ages seven to thirteen. Researchers found that overweight and obesity increased steadily from 1930 until the 1950s, reached a plateau in the 1950 to 1960 period, and rose again rapidly after that. A Nobel laureate in economics and others have revealed similar evidence for adults over a much longer period. Thus for higher-income countries, we can look at the large increases that began in the 1970s or 1980s, but we don't have a lot of insight into the earlier periods. In contrast, the lower-income world was plagued with poverty, hunger, and malnutrition, and had only a small over-weight population until the last several decades.

That the poor are more overweight than the rich is a phenomenon we have lived with for decades in the United States and Western Europe. Obesity, heart disease, and diabetes are all problems of the poor much more than of the rich. In one study in the United States, we identified public and private recreation facilities over a large geo-graphic area and calculated their distances from the homes of twenty thousand youths. We found that low-income and minority kids were much less likely to live within five miles of either public facilities such as parks, basketball courts, playgrounds, and YMCAs or pri-vate facilities such as gyms and pools. We also found that adding new facilities was associated with large decreases in the likelihood of obesity and large increases in being physically active.

The disparity in who receives the benefits of public funding— those who are poorer and need it more or those who are better off—is very important in creating a trajectory toward either a healthy or an unhealthy lifestyle. The more fortunate tend to begin life healthier and have greater access to both public and private facilities, affording them the opportunity to stay healthy.

Cesar Garcia is a perfect example of the problems that obesity can cause. Before his diagnosis, he had a number of difficulties— increased thirst, the need to urinate frequently, blurred vision, and fatigue—that became understood once his diabetes was confirmed by a local clinic. In the two months since, Cesar hadn't started taking his prescribed medication. As I previously mentioned, he worried about the cost of his medications because he didn't have adequate insurance to cover them. Moreover, he hadn't adjusted his diet, nor was he exercising. His situation will inexorably spiral out of control. Unlike Cesar, Bob Jones is taking medication for his hypertension, which has simpler (but still potentially fatal) complications.

Diabetics have a lower life expectancy and are vulnerable to critical problems that result from uncontrolled blood sugar levels, such as circulatory complications, nerve damage in the feet, poor vision, nausea, and weakness. More critically, diabetes can lead to heart disease, renal failure, and the loss of eyesight and limbs. Diabetics get sick for a long time before they die.

Unlike those born with type 1 diabetes, type 2 diabetics manufacture sufficient insulin, but the body's cells are resistant to its normal action. The passage of glucose through active muscle cells is restricted, resulting in excess glucose in the blood and urine. The body doesn't get the fuel it needs, and the buildup of glucose damages the blood vessels, nerves, kidneys, and eyes. One of the first major complications of those who don't control their diabetes is that their kidneys stop functioning. In the United States in the past thirty years, we've seen almost a tenfold increase in kidney failure, most of it due to uncontrolled high blood sugar. Many diabetics are unable to work. The life expectancy of a diabetic is reduced considerably, but more important, they become debilitated much earlier than people without diabetes.

Many of us know family members or friends of our families whose diabetes led to blindness and toe amputations. My mother's best friend was diabetic; she died two years ago from complications of the disease. Over the last fifteen years of her life she lost one toe after another and ultimately lost her ability to be mobile. When she died, she hadn't been able to walk on her own for some time, finally becoming wheelchair-bound.

My mother's death was also related to diabetes. At eighty-eight, she died a peaceful death in the summer of 2007. But in the two years before she died she went to the hospital eighteen times. She, too, was diabetic, though full-blown diabetes emerged only in the last two years of her life. However, excessive weight my mother put on over a long period beginning when she was in her fifties, high blood pressure, and diabetes ultimately destroyed her kidneys. In the last weeks of her life, her medical team finally said that there was nothing more they could do. She went into hospice care. Alleviating pain was then the key. Her family visited her; we ensured that a child or grandchild was there at all times. She got to eat all her favorite foods, and she spent her time regaling us with stories of her life. It was a joyous last two weeks. But it was the excessive weight, hypertension, and diabetes that eventually wore out her system.

A complex issue related to the rise in diabetes cases is that an increasing number of younger adults and teens are being diagnosed with adult-onset diabetes. We know that these young people do not do well with it. First, they show poor adherence to medical care; they lack the discipline required to properly manage their condition.

Second, they appear to more rapidly develop complications, such as the risk of heart attack. Studies have shown this same set of circumstances in Japan, Canada, and the United States. (Colleagues now tell me they find the same situation in Mexico, India, and other lower-income countries, but I haven't seen good research on the prevalence of the problem in these countries.)

Judging from the levels of obesity from 1984 to 2000 (which are lower than today), scholars estimate that about a third of men and almost 40 percent of women in the United States will have diabetes before they die. Of course, more recent research suggests that there is now a greater risk that U.S. residents will develop diabetes. The problem is much greater than predicted even five years ago. In fact, two studies done three to four years apart reveal how much greater this problem is. The first study estimated that in 2050 we would have 39 million cases of diabetes in the United States. However, the second study revised this estimate upward by 25 percent to 48.3 million cases of diabetes. My research shows that the rate at which Americans are becoming obese is increasing. I'd argue that this means we can expect to see continued upward revisions in the estimates of the number of cases of diabetes. In Canada, obesity is on the rise, as is diabetes.

Furthermore, it's very clear that if you have diabetes your risk of developing heart disease more than doubles. Because of the rise in diabetes, some scholars predict that we'll see an increase in deaths from heart disease in the future. From 1980 to 2000, deaths in the United States from heart disease decreased as a result of improved treatment and public health advances related to dietary changes and antismoking campaigns. But the increases in obesity and diabetes are expected to turn these promising numbers around.

And yet...there are solutions that can eliminate the need for medication. Two large trials undertaken in the United States and Finland show that a low-fat diet combined with increased activity and modest weight loss can reduce type 2 levels of diabetes in about 58 percent of adults. Asthma, hypertension, cancer, and sleep problems are also related to obesity. Globally, the numbers of adults and children who experience asthma is way up—some of this, to be sure, is caused by polluted air. In the United States, for instance, the proportion of children with asthma almost doubled between 1980 and 1996, to 6.2 percent of all children. Reports show that nearly 75 percent of emergency room visits for asthma were made by obese individuals, and studies reveal that obesity predates asthma.

When my paternal grandmother was in her sixties, she was overweight. I can understand why. Following years of poverty and hunger during her childhood in Eastern Europe and then during the decades after her family moved to the United States, she ate very rich food. Who could blame her? Of course, a downside is that she had hypertension. Today, conservative estimates indicate about one-quarter of the world's population—about a billion people—have hypertension.

Diabetes and the underlying hormonal changes related to it are linked with a number of cancers. A large team of eminent cancer scholars undertook a four-year, $6.5 million review of research linking lifestyle to cancer. Among their findings was a significant correlation of obesity and prevalence of body fat to breast, colon, endometrial, gallbladder, kidney, esophageal, and pancreatic cancers. Essentially, the major finding of this review was that *obesity is the most preventable cause of cancer.* (I'm a member of the policy component of this panel, so I saw how carefully and rigorously their criteria and conclusions were. This is the latest and best science on the subject to date.)

Sleep problems are also strongly linked with obesity. Extra body fat in the chest and neck constrict our air passages and even our lung functioning. Obese adults and teenagers have a great deal of trouble sleeping. Many studies show that obesity, particularly abdominal and upper body and neck obesity, is the most significant risk factor for obstructive sleep apnea. But we also find in human and animal research that reduced rapid eye movement (REM) sleep, a problem related to sleep apnea, may in turn increase the risk for obesity. Studies have found that animals deprived of REM sleep eat more. In addition, when people are tired they may exercise less. To compound things, sleep problems are strongly linked with heart disease.

Obviously, the global explosion of weight gain will make a much less healthy planet. Rich countries such as the United States can afford to have 15 to 20 percent of our national income spent on medical expenses. But there are many who argue that the government shouldn't be concerned about obesity because, unlike tuberculosis or AIDS, it isn't contagious. However, the health care costs of obesity are enormous and are reflected in the insurance rates the rest of us bear. In countries as diverse as China and India, the costs of obesity and nutrition-related, noncontagious diseases are the largest health-related costs these countries will face within the next fifteen years—if they aren't already.

Half a century ago in the United States, the only people who developed type 2 diabetes were in their late fifties or their sixties. Today, we are seeing type 2 diabetes emerge in childhood. Pediatric clinics and emergency wards, not only in the United States but also in countries as diverse as Australia, England, and Mexico, are seeing large proportions of adolescents—and even children—with type 2 diabetes. As I've mentioned, the two primary, preventable causes of type 2 diabetes are obesity and inactivity.

A Raleigh, North Carolina, doctor whom I talked with works in pediatric intensive care. He repeatedly sees heavy children coming in for emergency care. This might include, say, an obese teenage boy presenting with an asthma attack so severe that his heart has stopped, but more often than not the doctor sees children who are obese and have type 2 diabetes. Not long before I talked with him, one child had lingered before dying of type 2 diabetes complications. A case this severe is rare, but type 2 diabetes is not. When obese children develop asthma or diabetes, it will be with them for life. And of course, there are many other problems that accompany obesity that I've discussed above.

Two recent studies highlighted just how potentially serious the rapid increase in child obesity is. Aside from a few European countries, child obesity was pretty much an unknown problem in the world until the last half-century. Data from Denmark show precisely how obesity emerged in the 1920s and 1930s and has consistently grown until it began to rapidly increase in the 1980s and 1990s. In one recent study, we found that the rate of increase in child obesity was still slower than that for adults across the globe. Australia was the only high-income country where the rate of increase for children was higher than for adults. However, child obesity is now emerging in all countries of the world. We've found that 0.3 to 0.6 percent of all children are becoming overweight each year—a very troubling statistic.

Recently, these two studies appeared in *The New England Journal of Medicine*. As an editorial by the pediatrician David Ludwig noted, we might very well be underestimating the debilitating effects of child obesity. The two studies linked the risks of overweight or obesity in childhood and adolescence to heart disease in adulthood. One group studied the effect of being overweight or obese on the risk of heart disease at age twenty-five or older. They found the risk of a coronary heart disease event was strongly linked with the obesity of the child. As the children aged and became overweight or obese, the risk increased. The second study was a statistical analysis of the ways the current level of child obesity will translate by 2035 into increased adult obesity. These authors predict that the prevalence of coronary heart disease will have increased by 5 to 16 percent, with more than one hundred thousand excess cases attributable to increased obesity among today's adolescents. Ludwig and his collaborators have estimated that current levels of pediatric obesity may shorten life expectancy in the United States by two to five years by midcentury—an effect equal to that of all cancers combined.

I think that these reduced life expectancy figures are underestimations. Child obesity today is more severe than child obesity a decade ago. What this means is that today's children will be fatter than today's adults who were obese fifteen years earlier. The health effects of today's childhood obesity will be more serious, including coronary heart disease, liver disease, kidney difficulties, and a wide number of health conditions that will affect the health and quality of life of these teens and children.

In a nutshell, those are the health problems facing our fat world. What are the solutions?

For severe obesity, we have few effective treatments. But we know that surgery works. As we've seen, when a person is extremely overweight and is unable to lose weight, the health, social, and economic consequences are likely to be very serious. Some—if not most—who are excessively overweight have difficulty moving and therefore have few options for cutting their weight and preventing further disability and illness. For them, gastric bypass surgery is an effective option—if there is money to pay for it. In higher-income countries we recommend the surgery for obese men and women who have body mass indexes (BMI) of 35 along with coexisting illnesses such as diabetes. The surgery is also recommended for adults with a BMI of 40 or over, no coexisting illness necessary.

BMI is a measure of body roundness. It's a crude approximation of the amount of our body fat. (In clinical practice we use additional measures to understand if someone is overweight.) There are many Web sites where one can plug in their weight and height to learn their BMI. Obesity is a condition where there is excess body weight due to an abnormal accumulation of fat. A person with a BMI between 25 and 30 would be considered overweight. A BMI higher than 30 is the marker for obesity. At this point, we should expect some health and social consequences.

We are finding that race and ethnicity matters when it comes to BMI and diabetes. In what we call abdominal obesity, there is more fat around the heart and liver in Asians and Hispanics than among whites with the same BMI. A great deal of research shows that even for low BMIs, such as 20, South Asians from India have extensive body fat around these critical organs. They also have an obesity-linked increased likelihood of becoming diabetic. If you are an American of Mexican origin with a BMI of 22, you're more likely to develop diabetes than an American of Western or Eastern European origin with a BMI of 26 or 27. For children, BMI standards vary with age, gender, and maturational status. But an adult or child born of Hispanic or Asian descent will be much more likely to have abdominal obesity than a non-Hispanic white counterpart with the same BMI.

About 5 percent of American adults have a BMI over 40, what many call extreme obesity, and nearly one-third—that's about 61 million people—are obese with a BMI over 30. Thus, depending on the criteria we use, there are 20 million to 40 million Americans who should consider being evaluated for gastric bypass surgery. A major study from Sweden published in *The New England Journal of Medicine* followed gastric-bypass surgery patients. It suggested that weight loss resulting from the surgery is linked with reduced hypertension, reduced type 2 diabetes, and longer lives, among other benefits. (This study was based on surgery performed with an older, more complicated method. A newer, safer laparoscopic approach reduces postoperative recovery and is less stressful.)

Undergoing gastric bypass surgery is not simple, however, and requires both skilled surgical teams and follow-up assistance to ensure that patients learn to reduce portion sizes and follow healthy dietary guidelines. The economic costs of this surgery are very high, but the research done by the Swedes and subsequently by American scholars show that it is cost-effective. That is, the savings in reduced health problems offset the costs of the surgery. As Medicare has learned, gastric bypass is a wise use of government dollars.

Some scientists have shown that obesity runs in families and, hence, that it is a genetic disease. Other scholars, such as one set of British scientists, find that people who inherit one version of a gene called "FTO"—for "fatso"—are 70 percent more likely to be obese. (Despite its name, the true function of FTO remains unknown.) These scholars carefully note that FTO will not be the only gene that influences obesity, and that inheriting a particular variant will not necessarily make anyone fat. Additionally, people with the genetic variant may be slim unless they overeat or don't exercise. In other words, this gene may contribute to a risk of being overweight, but does not in and of itself cause obesity.

The respected *New York Times* science writer Gina Kolata is among those who believe that obesity is biologically determined. She argues that as a result of our genetics it is next to impossible to lose weight and that it is futile to try. She strongly supports Jeffrey M. Friedman's pathbreaking research on leptin, a hormone that is important in regulating body weight, metabolism, and even reproductive function. Some hope that it's a magic bullet. Researchers in England are giving leptin to rats during pregnancy and lactation, and they're finding that the infant rats are more resistant to obesity. These researchers are seeking patents for this approach; they see leptin as a possible antiobesity formula or drug.

While there might be a genetic predisposition to obesity, these genes won't kill us. Diet, inactivity, and energy imbalance are what kill us. And changes to these can and often do override genetics—if the changes are large enough. Nurture does trump nature. Essentially, I believe (as do most scientists) that a positive energy balance is necessary to acquire body fat. It is the persistence of this positive energy balance—that is, more food consumed than energy expended in calorie terms—that creates obesity over a longer time period. There is no way that genes, leptin, or other hormones, or even components of our diet such as sugar and refined carbohydrates, can cause obesity without creating a positive energy balance.

We know that it takes thousands of years for genes to change while, in fact, the obesity increases we have seen have taken place only in the past century in the higher-income world and in the past one to two decades in developing countries such as China. We are fat because food interacts with our genes to make us overweight. For these reasons, then, the argument that obesity is genetic, put forward by Kolata and others, seems naïve—or perhaps it's just a tiny piece of a much larger story.

I think that the shift to calorically sweetened beverages, larger portion sizes, more eating occasions, and the increased availability of sweeter and fattier foods—which are a result of technological and economic changes—are causing the obesity epidemic, not genes per se. Today, we are eating, drinking, and moving in ways unprecedented in human history. These changes have interacted with our biology to create the obesity epidemic—and all the individual and public health problems that go with it. It's quite possible that some of us have protective genes that interact with these environmental changes, making us less susceptible than others. Whatever the case, the full impact of genes will take a very long time to explain.

(Some who acknowledge that our DNA and RNA cannot change quickly do argue that the ways these genes express themselves might, and that these epigenetic changes are important. But nothing will change the law of energy balance—we must ultimately consume more calories than we expend to become overweight.)

Kolata is just one of many prominent voices pushing for medical approaches to cure obesity. And, in fact, many pharmaceutical companies are spending tens of millions of dollars searching for a magic obesity drug. But as we learn more about the complexity of the systems controlling food intake, energy expenditures, and energy balance, this goal seems ever more elusive and difficult.

The newest game in town involves shots that will "dissolve" body fat. This is perhaps the latest in the scary world of what I often feel is physician quackery. There are always a few who will use untested treatments and techniques to earn a buck. This is *not* the same as liposuction, where some of the fat on a patient's stomach, hips, chin, or face is surgically removed. Rather, the procedure called lipodissolve uses injections to target unwanted fat deposits, usually in the waist, thighs, or chin. These injections use ingredients such as phosphatidyl choline, multivitamins, deoxycholate, enzymes, and plant extracts, and also nonsteroidal anti-inflammatory medications, antibiotics, and hormones. The combinations of these elements, each of which in and of itself might seem harmless, could be very dangerous. Since these drugs are approved separately by the government as legitimate compounds, the FDA allows doctors to prescribe them. This is how the providers of lipodissolve obtain their mixtures. An example is Fig., a chain of fifteen centers across seven states, including three clinics in St. Louis. From 2006 to 2008, Fig. offices performed more than one hundred thousand lipodissolve treatments, as Chris Dornfeld, the company's chief development officer, stated in an interview for an article in *The New York Times*.

These antifat injections have not been studied, however, and there is as yet no standardization of the drugs used to dissolve and liquefy the fat. Nor do we know what the long-term consequences are. Early reports and studies cite bacterial infection, disfiguring masses of chronically inflamed tissue, localized tissue death, and other causes of skin discoloration. But because these approaches and drugs are not FDA approved (the individual drugs or ingredients are, but not their combination), there is no standardized data collection under way on this controversial new therapy. Brazil banned one of the substances used in lipodissolve because so many nonmedical professionals were using it and the complication rates were high. Doctors in Kansas and Missouri have been fighting to ban these drugs and this procedure. But systematic data are lacking; there have been no randomized controlled trials with placebos. British health authorities have issued consumer warnings, but no regulations exist in what is an unfettered arena where the beauty needs of the public may intersect with potentially dangerous "medicine."

This is just one recent example of how unscrupulous surgeons and physicians profit from those seeking to lose weight or remove unsightly fat. These are also reasons why much more aggressive, independent government oversight of the diet sector is needed. This use of a combination of approved ingredients or drugs occurred with disastrous consequences when doctors combined fenfluramine and phentermine into a weight-loss combination called Fen-Phen. The resulting drug worked wonders. Eighteen million prescriptions were written in a single year, 7 million Americans took this drug, and people lost large amounts of weight. But the drug combination created a heart condition that killed more than 150 people and caused lasting heart damage in thousands before it was banned by the FDA.

If there is no pill—or other magic bullet—we must ask whether the food industry can do anything about the problem.

6

Nothing to See Here: The Food Industry's Role in Causing and Solving the Problem

D r. John Harvey Kellogg (1852–1943) was a Seventh-day Adventist who opened a well-known hospital called the Battle Creek Sanitarium. Actually, it was more like a health resort than a hospital. At Battle Creek, for example, Kellogg taught about food preparation, had his clients engage in breathing exercises and marching to promote digestion, and he gave guests daily enemas and had them consume yogurt afterward.

Seventh-day Adventists have long practiced a vegetarian lifestyle. This led Kellogg to develop high-fiber, grain-based foods that would be both nutritious and palatable for patients. These included a cereal-based coffee substitute (he thought caffeine was bad for his patients' health), a patent for peanut butter (he thought nuts were a very important health food), and a cereal made from whole grains. Kellogg's sanitarium regimen had quirks, from the ridiculous to the appalling (e.g., patients receiving five enemas a day from a high-volume enema machine, as well as electric shock and laugh therapy), but the rich and famous, including Thomas Edison, Upton Sinclair, and Henry Ford, visited it during its twenty years of existence. The sanitarium offered its clientele a lifestyle of exercise and strict diet that prohibited alcohol, tobacco, and meat.

John Kellogg's first great invention was cornflakes, the result of experimentation in the 1890s. The sanitarium kitchen's cooked wheat was exposed to air for a day or more. Then, when running it through rollers, separate flakes were discharged and cereal flakes were born. The breakfast staple became an instant hit at the sanitarium and beyond, as guests would write after their visits to request supplies of their food.

Somewhere along the line this dream changed. The realities of selling cereal globally transformed Kellogg's into a company that produced a large array of products with refined carbohydrates, added sugars, and fats. The original cereals were made only with whole wheat and contained a small number of calories and plenty of fiber. But that was then—at less than 100 calories per serving—and this, at 120 to 400 calories per serving, is now. The virtuous company that made truly healthy products is a dim memory. Even so, Kellogg's, Post, and the other ready-to-eat cereals are a lot healthier than most breakfast alternatives such as bacon, sausages, and fried eggs.

Another example of this kind of change in the food industry is the Coca-Cola Company. It's remarkable that Coke originated as a health product, created by someone with ties to the world of medicine. While Kellogg was a physician, a pharmacist created Coke, as we saw in Chapter 2. Developed and sold as the "Great American Drink that eases nerve racking and physically exhausting terrors," Coke began as a patent medicine. Ubiquitous advertising, along with master mythmakers and shrewd businessmen, has taken Coca-Cola a long way beyond the vision of its founder, Dr. John Stith Pemberton (a pious Methodist who was dependent on morphine and later on his cola).

Kellogg's, Coke, and the entire food and beverage industries have been transformed.

For a long time with regard to obesity, the food industry seemed to be far more active trying to deflect focus from itself rather than dealing directly with the problem. There were, of course, a few important exceptions, even among industry giants as we'll see. But now major global companies are beginning to make big changes. There is, however, only so much companies with a conscience can do within a capitalist system that allows competitors who don't care about good health to undercut the good intentions and actions of their rivals.

The International Life Science Institute (ILSI), a food industry organization, was created in the United States in 1978 and expanded globally under the astute leadership of Alex Malaspina, the international vice president of Coca-Cola. This visionary felt the industry needed a common voice to address issues of food safety and toxicology, and to provide linkages with academic nutrition. Malaspina was very wise and also very protective of his own company; he tried hard to get the industry to focus on reduced physical activity as the cause of the obesity crisis. As a result, the food industry helped to fund and develop a number of major initiatives around physical activity. Some excellent physical activity programs have emerged, such as the Step Diet Program. This program, developed by the eminent nutritionist Dr. Jim Hill (a colleague and friend), encourages people to use a pedometer to count their steps and to make permanent changes in the amount of walking they do. He used this approach to cofound America on the Move, a national weight-gain prevention initiative that aims to get Americans to make small changes in how much they eat and how much they move.

While the ILSI might have started as a way to link industry, academia, and government, in reality it has become a voice for the food industry and, oftentimes, for Coca-Cola or the beverage industry. In the early 1990s, I traveled to China with ILSI's president as part of an international team that was to start a fortification program to eliminate iron-deficiency anemia and other nutrient deficiencies in China. I was working for an international organization called the Micronutrient Initiative; the others were there for ILSI. Traveling on the plane with us was a well-regarded Canadian nutritionist, Dr. Harvey Anderson, who was brought to China at the invitation of the ILSI president to discuss the sugar issue with Chinese colleagues and officials. In an earlier meeting in coastal China, my long-term Chinese collaborators and other scholars were creating Chinese dietary guidelines and one of them quipped that maybe the instruction to "reduce sugar intake" should be added to the guidelines. Since China has the lowest intake level of added sugar in the world, this was actually a joke. But to ILSI this was very serious. They have fought long battles seeking to get the scientific community to think of sugar as equivalent to any other carbohydrate—to consider a gram of sugar as no different from, say, a gram of whole grain. Neither Dr. Malaspina nor Dr. Anderson understood that sugar was a nonissue until after they arrived in Beijing and I relayed to them what my Chinese colleagues had told me. They had come all this way for no reason—except perhaps to underscore how important ILSI felt it was to prevent any regulation or education about the role of sugar in our diet.

A few years ago, I was invited to an ILSI conference to make a presentation on patterns and trends in the consumption of carbohydrates. Over the years ILSI has organized a number of these conferences in the United States; the major focus and purpose is to show that a calorie is a calorie, and a calorie of sugar is no different from a calorie of any other refined carbohydrate. I responded that I would love to attend, but felt it was important that, in my presentation, I raise some of the key public health controversies that result from this ILSI perspective—particularly concerns about how soft drinks and other calorically sweetened beverages affect obesity. I wanted to discuss the point that a calorie of sugar in a beverage is not treated by the body in the same way as a calorie of food but rather is ignored, so that when we drink sugared beverages, we're simply adding excess calories. I was immediately disinvited.

The ILSI may be promoting physical activity as one of the major ways to address obesity, but we know that, on average, daily caloric intake is increasing in our country. It's much easier to cut 10 to 100 calories from one's diet than it is to burn off the equivalent amount of calories through exercise. The America on the Move program is great and increasing physical activity is really important—but the food industry also needs to focus on the impact of its own behavior.

Having seen the ILSI in action for a long time, I've learned to be cautious of the way the food industry operates. For example, the industry makes an effort to co-opt professional nutrition and health associations, such as the American Dietetic Association, the American Heart Association, and others that I discuss below.

The American Dietetic Association is funded by many food companies and, I argue, views nutrition through the lens of the food industry. As the accrediting body for registered dietitians and university programs, the association has a great deal of power over its profession. At a pivotal time for the health of the nation, and when many scholars are identifying the negative effects of sugary beverages on health, this association has been working with the soft drink industry and ignoring the negative effects of their products. Many of its statements essentially place all beverages into the same category, viewing Coke, Pepsi, or juice as equivalent to water in terms of health effects. For instance, the American Dietetic Association's position on sugars in our diet echoes that of the food industry and differs from the World Health Organization's recommendation that only 10 percent of our calories should come from caloric sweeteners. The

American Dietetic Association accepts a 25 percent level, stating that "sweeteners elicit pleasurable sensations with (nutritive) or without (nonnutritive) energy.... By increasing palatability of nutrient-dense foods/beverages, sweeteners can promote diet healthfulness.... Scientific evidence [does not support] that intakes of nutritive sweeteners by themselves increase the risk of obesity." In a rather casual way, the American Dietetic Association follows outdated U.S. dietary guidelines regarding soft drinks and caloric beverages when the science is far more advanced. At a time of great interest in and controversy about the role of soft drinks in our schools and our lives—and with numerous meta-analyses and other studies on this topic—they have retained old, and what I think are somewhat dangerous, health guidelines. They often cite industry-funded studies but seldom cite opponents of their positions and meta-analyses. This organization uses research biased toward the food company or industry that is funding them. To me, it appears that the commercial side often blinds the scientific side no matter how well-meaning and professional are the individual members in the organization.

The American Heart Association (AHA), like a few other major nonprofit organizations, endorses products that fit its definition of being healthy—in the AHA's terms these would be "heart-healthy" food products. Yet the AHA receives for each product funds from the food company involved. Not surprisingly, products the AHA endorses include, dubiously, sugary cereals such as Frosted Shredded Wheat and Cocoa Puffs.

There is a distinct bias in research where the authors have been funded by the relevant food industry sector or have financial interests in their results. Two very large, carefully done reviews have studied the role of industry funding in obtaining possibly biased research results. One study just looked at the different findings in soft drink and obesity studies that were funded by the beverage and sugar industries. A second large meta-analysis of beverage studies looked across a range of questions to see how a source of funding might reflect bias in the results. In both papers the authors showed that the source of funding was linked with the outcomes. If a scholar received industry funding, he or she was much more likely to find a result that made the product involved look healthier. These kinds of results, for example, are why the dairy industry can tell us that milk consumption can lead to weight loss and how the beverage companies can claim that soft drink intake doesn't lead to obesity and diabetes. But if the funding came from the National Institues of Health (NIH) or from a source not linked to the product being studied, the results were much less likely to be favorable to the commodity or product involved. Of course, there are gaps in our knowledge and there will always be questions about the results when only one study is examined. However, these two papers reveal—based as they are on hundreds of studies—a large and systematic bias.

I think that an ethical line is crossed when scholars actively consult with companies and help to sell their products. The most blatant case is when a scholar holds a patent that he will gain from when a claim is made or a food, drug, or drink is consumed.

An interesting example of this problem starts with a well-meaning and influential group, the William J. Clinton Foundation. The Clinton Foundation created the Alliance for a Healthier Generation in a partnership with the American Heart Association. Our former president started this foundation with laudatory goals, one of which was to end child obesity.

I want to show how this effort ended up with unintended—and not completely healthful—consequences. The Clinton Foundation and the American Heart Association teamed with the American Beverage Association (and its founders—Coca-Cola, Pepsi, and Cadbury Schweppes) to create school beverage guidelines. They didn't involve scholars or activists who are trying to address the problems in schools and elsewhere that relate to beverages, health, and obesity. The American Heart Association does have a nutrition committee but it, too, wasn't involved (according to discussions I had with members of the AHA Nutrition Committee). In their desire to create joint guidelines, the Clinton Foundation, the AHA, and the American Beverage Association provided the companies with what I would call cover. The guidelines allowed for unrestricted portions of sports drinks and fruit juice in vending machines in the schools. The guidelines did ban soft drinks from elementary schools and did have many strong elements, but they went only halfway to what most health professionals involved with child obesity are seeking.

At this same time scholars, through a large body of research, were attacking these beverages and their availability in the schools. Moreover, a number of states and metropolitan areas had banned some of these items, and activist groups across the nation worked to get sports drinks out of all schools and to get fruit juice either eliminated or limited to small portion sizes. A number of National Academy of Science Committee publications had also discussed this topic. One focused on the broader issue of child obesity. Another focused on beverages and foods in the schools.

Contrasting the joint Clinton Foundation, AHA, and American Beverage Association guidelines are those of the Institute of Medicine of the National Academies. The Institute of Medicine is the only advisory body that is usually completely outside food politics, and the beverage component of its report involved very strong independent scholars who truly understood the issues. Its guidelines state that schoolchildren of all ages should drink only water—without flavoring, additives, or carbonation. The only two milk types recommended were low-fat 1 percent milk and nonfat skim milk. They limit the amount of sugar in flavored milks, though perhaps not enough. The panel also recommended portion controls: four-ounce portions of fruit juice for elementary- and middle-school students and eight-ounce portions for high school students. These recommendations are admirable and would indeed eliminate many calories for those children who obtain beverages at school. This model also provides an important example for America in general.

These guidelines became much more important in 2007 as the Senate and House Agricultural Committees attempted to finalize the school food and beverage standards component of the U.S. Farm Bill. It contains a section that standardizes beverage and snack rules for schools in an effort to begin addressing the issue of child obesity. Suffice it to say that the beverage industry, through its lobbyists in the American Beverage Association, attempted to promote its own guidelines, similar to those of the American Heart Association and Clinton Foundation. The Beverage Association guidelines for high schools essentially allow everything, including full-sugared soft drinks: diet sodas, sports drinks, caffeinated beverages, unlimited juice, and flavored and sugar-sweetened milk that contains 50 percent more calories than a Coke or a Pepsi. The danger of "guidelines" that attempt to salvage what they can on their members' behalf is best revealed by looking at Australia, the country with the fastest-growing child obesity on the planet. Here, schoolchildren consume almost no soft drinks but are permitted unlimited fruit juice, which contains hundreds of calories. America could become the next Australia, if we let the American Beverage Association have its way. Should we ban one sugared beverage only to have it replaced by another?

I think this is poor political strategy on the part of the beverage industry. Historically the proportion of children who purchased full-sugar soft drinks from school vending machines in schools is quite small. However, in fighting to keep these beverages in schools, the industry risks creating a much larger group of angry parents and citizens who will work for the larger common good and work for even tighter controls. It's possible that anger against the industry might ultimately lead to greater regulations. In the late 1970s the Nestlé company learned that sometimes it's wiser to listen to public opinion and move on when the stakes are small. Nestlé chose to sue the Third World Action Group, which published a pamphlet titled *Nestlé Kills Babies,* about the marketing and use of Nestlé infant formula in low-income countries. While Nestlé won the two-year trial, the publicity surrounding the lawsuit helped activists to begin a worldwide boycott. The boycott blew up into a major global issue and public relations nightmare for Nestlé. Even though Nestlé won the battle in court, the company was tagged as a baby killer, affecting their public image and sales for a long time.

The Snack Food Association operates much like the American Beverage Association. The Snack Food Association also worked with the Clinton Foundation to endorse recommendations that run somewhat counter to those of the Institute of Medicine. The Clinton Foundation, working again with the American Heart Association and the Snack Food Association, created school snack guidelines. These guidelines essentially still allow kids to eat all the junk food they'd been enjoying—including chips and doughnuts—but got the snack food companies who were members of the association to limit the amount of calories per package and to slightly rebalance the nutrient composition. In contrast, the Institute of Medicine's recommendations ban all potato chips, doughnuts, and other junk food and promote much healthier snacks, including whole grain products, fruits, and vegetables.

Yet even the most conscientiously articulated guidelines have problems. As Walt Willett pointed out, the Institute of Medicine does not allow all potentially healthy foods to be available. He noted in a letter that some "very healthy foods, like unfried nuts and seeds, probably peanut butter sandwiches, and entrée salads with dressing [are] excluded," while many junk and heavily sweetened foods remain. In preparing its recommendations, the Institute of Medicine perhaps concluded that because nuts, seeds, and salad oils have excessive calories, they should be discouraged. This might be correct, but it shows there is always the possibility of disagreement when it comes to even the best-crafted consensus. And thus, only after we test the effects of these guidelines, including the far more lax recommendations urged by the Clinton Foundation–Alliance for a Healthier Generation, will we know if they work. One issue is that all these snack food guidelines are focused on what should not be allowed rather than focusing on what *should* be allowed—whole-grain products, fruits and vegetables, and low-calorie items, none of which should be fried.

In addition, many of the professional associations have endorsement policies and receive a great deal of money to endorse various products. The American Diabetes Association is most focused on sugar, so it endorses products without sugar. That's good, but when deciding what to endorse it ignores calories—which is not good. The American Heart Association is concerned with saturated fat, salt, and trans fats; it focuses on reducing the intake of foods with these ingredients. However, it too ignores the calorie content in the products it endorses, such as a chocolate mousse drink with 140 calories (including 116 calories of sugar), high-calorie fruit juices, and others. The American Diabetes Association will support SnackWell's, a product that purports to be healthy and that contains minimal saturated fat but a great deal of sugar and calories. (SnackWell's sandwich crème cookies contain about 2,520 calories in a 20.4 ounce package versus 2,400 calories in an eighteen-ounce package of Oreo sandwich cookies.) The American Diabetes Association received so many complaints and adverse press that it revised its guidelines for what foods it will endorse. Even so, one must remain wary. The Diabetes Association has signed dozens of agreements, including a $1.5 million sponsorship deal with Cadbury Schweppes that allows that company to use the American Diabetes Association logo on many of its products. The American Heart Association and the American Dietetic Association are no different. The public needs to be vigilant about who is endorsing what.

Currently, Big Sugar and Big Beverage are the closest things to Big Tobacco and the way that for decades they promoted their case and protected their interests. Big Tobacco has always used legal and lobbying techniques as well as the research of tobacco-oriented scientists to attempt to thwart restrictive, antismoking legislation across the globe. For example, in 2003 the sugar and beverage industries tried to stop a major report coming from a joint World Health Organization and Food and Agriculture Organization panel. As part of the draft "Technical Report: Diet, Nutrition and the Prevention of Chronic Diseases," the panel recommended that only 10 percent of a person's daily calories come from added sugar.

A huge uproar followed. First, the president of the U.S. Sugar Association sent a private letter to the World Health Organization director-general, Gro Harlem Brundtland, in which he asked the organization to remove the sugar guideline. Dr. Brundtland, in turn, made the letter public. This letter warned that the Sugar Association would "exercise every avenue available to expose the dubious nature" of the WHO's report on diet and nutrition, including cessation of the $406 million in funding from the United States. The letter noted that "taxpayers' dollars should not be used to support misguided, non-science-based reports that do not add to the health and well-being of Americans, much less the rest of the world." It went on to say: "If necessary we will promote and encourage new laws which require future

WHO funding to be provided only if the organization accepts that all reports must be supported by the preponderance of science."

The Sugar Association and several American beverage companies also wrote to the then U.S. secretary of health and human services Tommy Thompson, asking him to use his influence to have the WHO report withdrawn. A coalition comprising more than three hundred companies lobbied him. In 2003, after both Deputy General Director Derek Yach and Gro Brundtland had left the WHO, another letter was sent from William R. Steiger, the special assistant to the secretary of health and human services, to the new director-general, Dr. Lee Jong-Wook. This letter focused on other issues in the report that U.S. food companies—and the U.S. Department of Health and Human Services as their spokesperson—wanted changed, including comments on the adverse effects of fast-food restaurants on diets. The department also denied a connection between products such as soft drinks and obesity.

Later, various groups reviewed and criticized the WHO report, including the Confederation of Food and Drink Industries of the European Union, the European Vending Association, the Food and Drink Federation, the Grocery Manufacturers of America, the International Soft Drinks Council, the International Sugar Organization, the Mauritius Ministry of Agriculture, the National Food Processors Association, Queensland Sugar Limited, the Republic of the Philippines Sugar Regulatory Administration, the South African Cane Growers Association, the South African Sugar Association, the Sugar Association, Inc., the Swaziland Sugar Association, the Thai Sugar Millers Corporation Limited, and the World Sugar Research Organization. The list goes on. It reads like a Who's Who of the sugar world.

But the disputed report was ultimately published. In this case, the industry's strong-arm tactics backfired, as so many of its lobbying tactics and letters were made public.

Some time ago, I was uncertain as to whether there were any good companies when it came to the global fight against obesity. But I've come to see that there are some companies doing good for the world's health. I have also seen major changes in companies like Coca-Cola and McDonald's.

In March 2007, I was in Europe to present some of my research on water and obesity reduction to executives and researchers from the Danone Research Center in Paris. Danone and Nestlé are the major global bottled water companies. I wanted them to create a joint research fund to support research on water and obesity and diabetes—a neglected area in obesity research. In the midst of the discussion, the nutrition team told me how they had been systematically reducing the sugar content in their product line each year. They would start with one product and quietly reduce its added sugar and calorie content each year, but never tell their customers. In fact, they worried that if they told their customers, the consumers would be unhappy and demand their sugar back in order to get their "money's worth." I pushed them hard to show me the facts. The company provided me with confidential data confirming its sugar reduction in beverages. (For example, the data showed Danone reducing over several years the sugar content of each type of sweetened water by 20 to 40 percent of its original calorie value for products in five or six countries.)

In another example of corporate responsibility, Kraft Foods has stopped advertising some foods to children. Kraft has been trying to learn from the experience of its sister company, Philip Morris USA (both are owned by Altria). Kraft has been attempting to be proactive rather than deny that a problem exists. The company has been meeting with its critics and trying to make suggested changes.

Kraft has also cut the sugar it adds to many of its food products. For instance, it created a sugar-free Oreo with just 50 calories per cookie. In 2005, Kraft cut the sugar in Post Honeycomb cereal to 10 grams from 12 grams. But are these reductions enough? We'll have to see; we don't yet know the health benefits of such changes.

Many other global food companies have joined Kraft in this effort. General Mills has created strict internal standards on what it regards as healthy products. Reducing calories, creating only whole-grain cereals, and reducing sodium, saturated fats, and trans fats are some of its initiatives. General Mills is not only working to make its entire product line healthier, it is also putting visible total-calories-per-serving labels on the front of each box. This creates an incentive for the food industry to cut added sugars whether they are natural sugar, high-fructose corn syrup, fruit juice concentrates, or other caloric sweeteners. Kellogg's is also now trying to reduce the calorie content of many of its cereals. Moreover, these companies are not advertising all of their changes.

Many food companies are now trying to position themselves as the "healthy" company. Some like Danone or Nestlé, with water, coffee, tea, milk, yogurt, or other potentially healthful items, might be in the best position to claim this mantle. But during the last few years I've found many others who are trying. Even Coca-Cola, so often seen as a major bad guy—by me and other scholars and activists—is working hard to shift its product line so that more of its total product mix is from noncalorie and very-low-calorie items. In Mexico, where I have been involved with the Ministry of Health in attempting to restrict use of caloric beverages, Coca-Cola didn't fight many new restrictions. Along with some other global food companies, they kept the national food and beverage company trade association from fighting in the media and in Congress against the new beverage guidelines. Of course, I'd like to see Coca-Cola cut the calories in all its drinks to truly enhance health, but this might not be possible unless legislation created a level playing field so that all beverage companies have to do the same. I'll return to this below.

Unilever, maker of items such as Lipton's tea, Hellmann's mayonnaise, Wish-Bone dressings, and the Knorr brand, is one of the three largest global food companies, along with Kraft and Nestlé. Like Danone and others, it is working in a stealth manner to cut calories and added sugar in many of its products. So are infant food manufacturers Wyeth, Mead Johnson, and Gerber. They, too, are concerned about the added sugar content of their items and are planning to silently follow the slow and systematic Danone model.

There are other companies that are working with independent nutrition scholars to make changes that are beneficial to health. One of these is Delhaize America. This is a leading U.S. supermarket operator with more than fifteen hundred stores in sixteen states in the eastern United States. It includes the 161 Hannaford supermarkets in New England. In collaboration with scholars from the University of North Carolina, Hannaford developed a system called "Guiding Stars" that rates the nutritional value of most of the food and beverages sold in its stores. About twenty-seven thousand products have been rated, and of these, 72 percent received no stars. This included items claimed to be good for you, such as juice (which has too much sugar), whole milk (which has too much fat), and yogurt with fruit (which has too much sugar). Most fruits and vegetables, some cereals, salmon, and other items earned three stars. The Hannaford effort is striking in that it is rating all the products it is trying to sell, and so its financial interest is the same as that of the food companies. But Hannaford is trying to sell products by highlighting for consumers the foods that are better for us. The only weakness in the system, in my opinion, is that it bases its rating solely on food quality dimensions such as saturated fat and trans fat content, while it ignores the question of total caloric content. Furthermore, the rating is not done by product type and thus is much cruder than it should be. Some higher-calorie juices, therefore, slip through the cracks. However, Hannaford's focus on reducing saturated fats, trans fats, increasing fiber, and providing the overall nutrient profile of foods is an important model for what food companies, countries, and food markets can follow.

What is really fascinating is how consumers are responding to the Guiding Stars system. Data compiled for over one year, for example, showed a large shift toward poultry products with a star and a decline in those without one. This trend was replicated throughout the system. In other words, sales shifted significantly to those food items with the stars. Now the European-owned Delhaize is expanding this system to other U.S. chains it owns, such as Food Lion.

Delhaize, however, doesn't publish its criteria, which is unfortunate because companies can't improve their products to meet the criteria. The food industry, or at least many of the corporate giants, would like to rectify this. Led by companies like Unilever and Kraft, the major U.S. food industry companies want to work out a common, science-based system of what constitutes a healthy food. By the end of 2008 they'll end up with a system that rates products within product groupings (such as the oils and cereals groups). This is based on food components that are considered good for you, such as calcium and fiber, and components that should be limited, such as trans fats, saturated fat, added sugars, and sodium. Ultimately these food companies will need to run this by an independent group of experts who will revisit the criteria every three to four years. It's essential that these experts be seen as independent of the food companies. I'm optimistic that a simple system that is designed by eminent nutrition scientists and that considers diet quality—minimal trans fats, reduced sodium, high whole grains, limited added sugars, calorie limits, good fats—with a focus on obesity and other chronic diseases will be devised. If governments around the world legally required such a system, this would obviously be beneficial.

I'm involved in Choices International's Scientific Board, an effort to create such a system for countries across the globe. Mexico's Ministry of Health and groups that I work with in China and elsewhere are interested in the same types of systems. Out of this I hope will come a simple classification of foods that will assist consumers across the globe in making healthier food choices. These rating systems would encourage manufacturers to change their products to meet the standards required to be called a healthful food.

There are other positive steps that major food retailers are taking:

- Starbucks reduced the fat in all dairy products added to coffee by moving from whole milk to 2 percent milk. This is a small start, and we hope the chain will move to less fat in its milk even more quickly. Starbucks has also introduced the "skinny latte," which is based on nonfat milk with sugar-free syrup. This will have 90 calories versus the normal latte with almost 400 calories.
- T.G.I. Friday's created a "right portion, right price" promotion. That is, for many items it is now offering a small portion size for a cheaper price—and the company has gained profits in the process. Other restaurants are starting to offer small plates, mini-desserts, and similar options. A poll of twelve hundred chefs by the National Restaurant Association in both 2007 and 2008 put these mini-desserts at the top "What's hot" spot. But until all food companies push clear calorie labeling and have resealable bags and reusable containers that allow food and beverages to be consumed in smaller sizes, the fundamental idea of portion control won't

gain traction. And of course, as we have discussed, it is the fast-food world where we need to focus on this the most.

- 7-Eleven stores are promoting healthier choices and adding more fruits, vegetables, packaged salads, and portion- and calorie-controlled items.

- McDonald's added a huge salad lineup, reduced some portions, and in other ways is trying to move toward some healthier fare. In fact, McDonald's has done much more than that. It has made a major corporate strategy shift, taking the position that "better is more important than bigger." The company is focusing more on health and less on adding thousands of new stores each year. The introduction in 2007 of the Hugo—a forty-two-ounce, 410-calorie drink for eighty-nine cents—was a blunder that undermined the new strategy. Not only did McDonald's receive a lot of bad publicity from this, but two executives in charge of the company's health push told me that it was an error that slipped through and that it's being stopped.

- Disney is also trying to create healthy foods for its amusement parks that it will brand. Disney is eliminating trans fats from all the food served at its theme parks by the end of 2008. Kids' meals will include applesauce and carrots instead of French fries.

These important and forward-thinking strides aside, we must not forget that these companies aren't eliminating unhealthy fare or using favorable pricing and other approaches to truly shift consumer behavior. Furthermore, many of the items that they call "better for you" are really not better for you when judged by nutritionists. For instance, Pepsi calls its sports drinks better for you. When compared with soft drinks, sports drinks have half the calories—but this is still way too much. Pepsi also calls fruit juice a good-for-you food, but its calorie content is even greater than that of soft drinks.

It is also very difficult to make sustained progress in any of these areas unless all the competitors change at the same time. It's a major concern for companies that want to address the obesity issue, but whose competitors look at these moves as an opportunity to increase their market share.

The global food industry has great ability and strength. It can grow, buy, and distribute anything, anywhere. It can take vegetables or meat from a remote village in one country, ensure it adequate hygiene and refrigeration, and transport it safely to any destination on the planet in days. It handles perishable fruits, vegetables, dairy, and meat products in as sanitary a method as the world has ever seen. Wal-Mart, Carrefour, and the other global food super marketers can handle and process food far more efficiently than any government.

Advertising, packaging, and distributing—rather than the ingredients themselves—make up most of the cost of food. The cost of ingredients often makes up only 5 to 10 percent of a processed food's retail price. For soft drinks, the ingredients cost pennies. The markup is thus enormous; food producing and processing is a hugely profitable and powerful enterprise.

Why, then, is the industry unable to work together to encourage people to eat less and drink less, and to consume a healthy diet? It could do that and still profit—or could it?

The food industry is rife with oligopolies—a few companies dominate the market. For instance, Coke, Pepsi, and Cadbury Schweppes dominate the beverage market, and each firm influences the others. McDonald's, Burger King, Wendy's, and Hardee's dominate the fast-food hamburger industry. Now, take the situation in which

McDonald's tries to do something beneficial to health by introducing lower-calorie salads and reducing the portion sizes of its beverages. But then Burger King and Hardee's introduce 1,000- to 1,400-calorie beverages and sandwiches. This would result in McDonald's losing some of the heavy-user market—the big eaters. As recently as the summer of 2007, Burger King and Hardee's continued introducing menu items with tons of calories and saturated fat. Burger King started selling the Ultimate Double Whopper—two quarter-pound beef patties topped with eight slices of bacon and four slices of American cheese—a 1,110-calorie message to consumers that health isn't important. This summer Wendy's introduced the 830-calorie Baconator. Unless food companies work together toward common goals concerning health, the public will lose.

When I read headlines like "World's Biggest 25 Food Companies Not Taking Health Serious Enough," as I did in 2006 when my friend Tim Lang published a report about the practices of the food industry, I think about my interactions with the many people in the food industry who do care. But I also think of the economic reality of the food industry, and I know that Tim is correct on the facts. Over a two-year period, Tim studied what each of the major food companies was doing to feed us better. According to his standards—which involve company policies and actions on research and development spending, marketing, advertisement, and policies on diet, activity, and obesity—they just weren't making big enough changes.

How do we unleash the good forces in the food industry? How do we get the food industry to help us reduce calories? Despite the many good things that some companies are doing, will we ultimately need regulations so that the entire industry acts toward the common goal of reducing obesity? What can individuals do about our global weight problem?

7

What Can We Do?

Obesity is so widespread and intractable an issue that it's hard to know how to move forward. However, my experiences dealing with poverty and hunger in the United States and India impressed upon me that individuals can make a major difference. It may not be easy, and big changes certainly don't happen quickly. Making changes in our communities, our children's schools, our churches, and our local and regional institutions is easier than making changes higher up the scale at the national and global levels. Nevertheless, change is possible at all levels.

Clearly, we can all make better choices that will help us to be thinner and healthier. My favorite way to help people lose weight is to look at what they drink over the course of a typical day. It's easy to cut out some Coke, Pepsi, or Mountain Dew, or to cut down to one beer or one glass of wine. These small reductions matter over time. If you need to lose a lot of weight for health reasons—if you're diabetic or if you've recently had a heart attack, for example—a shift to only noncaloric beverages will do it for most of us. The top 40 percent of caloric beverage drinkers in the United States consume over 760 calories a day from beverages. Obviously, cutting out some of those calories would result in immediate weight loss. Another option—one that has worked for me—is to eliminate desserts and chocolates for whatever length of time it takes for me to lose a few pounds, say a week or a month. As a chocoholic, this is difficult for me—but it works. Moving as much as possible also helps. Walk up and down stairs more, don't use elevators or escalators—just keep moving. As we've seen, a small amount of daily movement matters.

Of course, for lasting health there is a lot more we can and should do: eat lots of fruits and vegetables; cut out fried foods and fried snacks such as chips; work to shrink our stomachs (so that we need less food to feel sated) by cutting down portion sizes; and shift completely to whole-grain breads and cereals. We can eat Italian pasta, which is made from durum wheat, and get the same benefits as from whole wheat pasta made in the United States. Durum wheat contains a large percentage of high-quality protein. It's a big reason why the Mediterranean diets of Sicily and Italy in the 1950s and 1960s were so healthy.

We've all heard a cacophony of confusing, even ominous, messages about food from books, the media, and other sources. While these messages have the cumulative effect of reminding us to make good food choices, they can paralyze us as to how to go about it. We can—and must—agree on one thing: food matters. There are, however, many reasons why we don't understand what is in food. The supplement and food industries are both constantly selling us on the benefits of the newest processed food with this extra nutrient or that special substance that supposedly prevents cancer or heart problems and promotes wellness and longevity. In many ways, this is very sad, as it has distanced us from important truths about the food we eat and the combinations of food that make us healthy or unhealthy. We must stay away from food fads until clear research shows they are beneficial.

We must also stay alert to the fact that it's total calories that matter. Too many calories mean excessive energy intake. This leads to weight gain. Whether excess calories come from beer, Coke, or French fries doesn't matter. For example, we may crave the gustatory pleasure of Belgian chocolate as well as its heart-health benefits, but gaining twenty to thirty-five pounds in a year to get its health benefits is counterproductive.

What do we know? We know that the energy density of food is significant. In general, reducing energy density is a good thing. That is, if we consume foods that contain more fiber and water, such as most vegetables and fruit (or even soups when compared with stews), we'll eat less and be sated more readily. Therefore, if you eat a lot of fruit and vegetables you'll be much better off. (Of course, you can also consume too many calories from fruit and vegetables.) We know that protein fills us up faster, and that lean meat, tofu, fish, and other sources of protein are more filling. We know that some whole grains, with lots of fiber, are important, and that whether you eat a higher-fat or a lower-fat diet matters. It doesn't matter, however, whether the fat you eat comes from meat that is factory raised, from lard, or from other less healthy foods—it is still fat when we think about calories. For health the type of fat matters, however, as noted earlier. And we know that moderation, or portion control, is the secret. Reduced calories can come from any source.

Higher consumption of whole grains and fiber has consistently been linked in both randomized controlled trials and larger epidemiological studies with smaller waistlines and reduced weight. This is true across all age groups. As one careful review noted, "In both clinical trials and observational studies the intake of whole-grain foods was inversely associated with plasma biomarkers of obesity, including insulin, C-peptide, and leptin concentrations."

Frankly, it would be difficult for a person to be heavy if he or she drank only water, consumed a small amount of added sugar in foods, ate lots of fruits and vegetables, and ate no fried foods. Of course, one needs also to be physically active. To retain a high level of mobility as one ages, one must either walk a lot or do other, more aerobic physical activities. Sweating is good, and some lifting and muscle training is great. I realized only a few years ago how valuable it would be to have someone help me be active. I hired a trainer to show me how to strengthen my back and shoulder muscles. This completely changed me. My posture improved, and I learned to take my healthfulness to another level of well-being. But this isn't for everyone. Walking more, using the stairs each day, parking farther away in parking lots, and other small changes make a big difference over time.

For children, the secret is to start young. Offer them only healthy options. Keep a lot of cut-up fruit and vegetables available, try to give them water plus real fruit or packaged fruit—not bottled juices—and skim and 1 percent milk. Do not give them sweets, soft drinks, such things as chocolate- or strawberry-flavored milk, and other sugared foods that children become dependent on at a very early age. And if a child's friends drink soda and juice and go to fast-food restaurants? A friend told me that she would tell her children that if they were being taken to McDonald's by their friends (as part of a play date or birthday party) they needed to be respectful and polite. They could select carefully, or go with the flow, but with the understanding that at home, we don't eat this way. For my friend, this good modeling worked. Her kids are now much older, and never go to fast-food restaurants on their own.

Equally important is to encourage active play and to discourage long stretches of passive time spent in front of the TV or video gaming system or computer.

What Can We Do?

Motivation means so much. Individuals must want to make changes. Perception and self-image—how we view both ourselves and our children—matter, too. If we think that we are too heavy or in danger of becoming too heavy, we'll have the desire to change. If we truly understand that activity is important to be healthy, we'll encourage our family to be more active.

We need to realize that our perception of how much is too much has changed—for the worse. For example, an average American woman in 1994 thought her desired weight should be 132 pounds. By 2002 that figure had crept higher, to 135 pounds. Americans, even obese Americans, think their body weight is socially acceptable. With all the public concern over obesity we might ask why close to half of those who are obese think their body weight is not an issue. We might also ask why most doctors treat the problem, but don't promote prevention or healthy diets or activity. As a public policy question, part of the problem relates to the large proportion of us who don't have medical insurance and don't go to doctors for regular checkups or medical care. Also, we must take the fashion industry to task, which began to obscure the obesity issue in 1983 when it dropped the idea of standardization for sizing after it found that women returned to buy clothes more often if they were sized smaller, even though they were cut larger. Since then, smaller sizes have gotten bigger. This sly and pernicious changing of clothing sizes may have created more complacency among women.

Most parents don't realize when their child is obese or overweight. One recent national survey of parents found that more than 40 percent of parents with obese children ages six to eleven describe their child not as obese, but as "about the right weight." And this same poll found that only 13 percent of parents with obese children in that same age range rate their child as being very overweight, compared with 31 percent of parents with obese children ages twelve to seventeen. One of the first steps we can take is to make sure that pediatricians, school nurses, and society in general educates parents so they understand when their child is overweight or at risk of becoming overweight or obese.

Most important, for all children, is that changes begin with the family. The parents have to want to make changes—and to make changes for the entire family. Family change is the ideal way to help children change. There are dozens of successful examples of this such as interventions where the mother and the child or the entire family meet jointly to discuss making changes together. Teaching parenting skills also works—such as leaving healthy foods out for snacking; learning to say no to kids' requests for sugared cereals, flavored milks, soft drinks, and candy; and limiting the amount of TV to an hour a day or on Sundays only. In addition to healthy food choices, reducing passive, inactive time is key. All the research on children's food and beverage intake reveals that the parents must change first.

Many of my colleagues across the country are focused on helping parents learn to make better decisions about how both they and their children eat, drink, and move. At my obesity center, we have faculty fellows who work on parenting education. They work with parents to prevent and treat eating disorders. They work with low-income mothers to teach them how to change the food environment at home and the feeding of infants, toddlers, and older preschoolers. Good habits start at home, and start early in life.

Of course, this book is not just about individual choices. Our surroundings affect our choices, as do decisions at the community, state, national, and global levels. For each individual who is trying to lose weight, there are many stimuli around them that encourage constant eating and drinking. Wherever we turn, food is available and promoted; and it's cheap, it's tasty, and it's something social to do. The addition of sugar and fat increases the allure of foods. Perhaps what is most surprising is that more of us aren't overweight—although, as you're well aware, I argue that we are heading in that direction.

What can each of us do to promote change in our environment so that we move more and eat healthier food? Well, we can exercise our power as ordinary citizens by making our officials aware, through the ballot, that this is a major concern and that action is needed.

But there are many things we can do for ourselves and our families. First, we need to be sure that children have a safe way to walk to school. When my son was young, a group of neighborhood children would meet outside our homes and walk to school together. Luckily, the path to school was close by, safe, and didn't cross any dangerous streets. We parents felt comfortable with the children walking together. Nonetheless, there was always one or more of us watching them gather and go to school in a group. If, for some reason, my son was to go to school without his friends, we either went with him or didn't let him walk. Of course, many families don't live close enough to a school or in a safe enough neighborhood to make walking to school a possibility, but dozens of communities in the United States have been able to organize walk-to-school groups. These groups have found ways to organize parents so that one adult can walk with the children where there is traffic or to create other, safer ways for them to walk to school. Two colleagues conducted a national review of dozens of these programs to learn more about what methods might work. They found that "strong community involvement, some funding, repeat participation, and environmental audits are associated with programs that adopt environmental/policy change, and seem to facilitate walking to school."

Walking to school is one way to help children spend more of their day in movement. But parents need to push schools to have physical education classes that matter—PE classes during which kids are active and actually sweat. Beyond that, it's up to parents to find ways to keep kids moving by, say, encouraging their children to join intramural groups for team or individual activities and preventing too much passive activity such as watching TV and playing video games.

This takes a lot of effort and vigilance, given all the social signals and cultural pressures—such as ubiquitous advertising—that guide our children toward the latest junk foods. Moreover, none of this will work if the parents themselves are spending their afternoons and evenings in front of the TV. Parents need to be role models to their children, but also to walk and hike with them, and engage them in other active pursuits when they are young. For many adults, this means a change in routine and attitude.

Another thing we can do is support the funding of parks and the development of youth sports activities, including soccer, lacrosse, basketball, and, of course, many others. We can also support and promote preschool and after-school programs that encourage children to be physically active. A wonderful way to do this is through games such as Dance Dance Revolution (DDR). DDR is a video game that requires players to move rhythmically to music; as they're playing the game they're required to execute the proper steps on a dance pad. It's an extraordinarily popular game, and many elementary schools have purchased systems for their physical education classes and for use at lunchtime. We also need to focus attention on activities that encourage physical activity but that aren't competitive sports—such as wall climbing, jumping rope, dancing, nature walks, hiking, and biking—which are likely to be preferred by children who aren't athletically gifted. The next generation of these is Wii Fit, which also gets kids and adults to move.

Parents often tell me that they may be successful at limiting TV time, but that it's much more difficult to resist children's pressures about food. It's much easier to give a child a Coke than to ensure that he drinks milk and eats vegetables. However, we've found that if a child sees or is given only healthy options, he'll begin a lifetime of healthy eating and drinking. In fact, as my friend Susan Roberts of Tufts University shows in the book *Feeding Your Child for Lifelong Health*, providing healthy foods and resisting other requests may help get kids to eat right. Kids may complain or not eat the vegetables for a day or so, but they will give in. The same goes for beverages. A fussy child will complain or refuse, but stops quickly if the parent is resolute. Parents across the United States have been demanding better, fresher, and more nutritious food for our kids at school. However, we have to maintain the same standards at home. We might remember that most soft drinks and nutrition-poor snacks—fried foods, sweet baked goods, and such—come from our own kitchens. Parents need to be educated and—if they aren't already—we need to fund teachers, health educators, or others to help with this.

Two Connecticut mothers, Amy Kalfa and Susan P. Rubin, have started their own child advocacy organization. Included in their activities have been dozens of visits and talks at the local school board, a presentation at a special panel on child obesity at the National Institute of Medicine, and the production of a movie, *Two Angry Moms*. Armed with a movie camera, Amy and Susan visited school cafeterias to record what was on the menu. They met with food-service vendors, teachers, health experts, politicians, parents, and officials from the U.S. Department of Agriculture and the Food and Drug Administration. They analyzed the meals and proposed workable, equally inexpensive healthy options. Go to their website, angrymoms.org, to see a great example of what mothers can do. Their activities and results are inspiring.

Just as fantastic is an e-mail I recently received from a fifth-grade girl. She and her friends had created a group to get healthy food and beverages onto their school cafeteria's menu. They were having difficulty and asked for our help. Calling themselves "The Battle for a Better

Meal Group," they began circulating a petitition and were going to the principal, the school board, and others. Among other things, they complained that the reward for good grades at their school was Chick-fil-A or pizza. Go, girls!

Many schools and school boards have begun to restrict what parents are allowed to send to school with their children. Water, fruit, and vegetables are allowed, but no more chips, sweet stuff, and other junk foods. A number of districts have also started to limit snacks to one per day, have cut lunchroom portions, and only allow seconds on fruit, vegetables, and salad. Many of these initiatives began with parents raising the issue to school boards. In California, for instance, parent groups succeeded in banning all deep fryers from school cafeterias, so even chicken nuggets must now be baked. They, and other groups across the country, accept that these improvements require time and money. It costs more for schools and preschools to create healthy snacks of fruit and vegetables. It takes more time to prepare school breakfasts and lunches that contain less sodium and fat but more healthy proteins.

The USDA now requires each school to have its own nutrition and wellness policies, a development that empowers parents who care. And yet, there will be backlash. There will be parents who want their children to be able to purchase soft drinks at vending machines. For instance, when a school in England banned students from both buying soft drinks and bringing them from home, parents camped outside the school in protest. There will also be parents who don't want their kids labeled as "fat." This will likely be a long, slow struggle.

In addition to the cafeteria and vending machines, I should note that schools' fund-raising activities, as well as those of other groups like the Girl Scouts, are renowned for trying to get us to eat cookies, brownies, candy, and cupcakes—foods that are full of sugar and fat. One study showed that 76 percent of school fund-raisers sell chocolate, 67 percent sell baked goods, and 63 percent sell non-chocolate candy. As an alternative, parents can promote walkathons, car washes, environmental actions, healthy food sales, book fairs, and hundreds of other activities that bring in money but don't promote unhealthy eating and drinking.

But in an era in which school boards are looking for new revenue sources and also to provide incentives for better performance, there are troubling signs. Until adverse publicity put an end to this practice in January 2008, McDonald's restaurants in Seminole Country, Florida, and the Seminole County School Board agreed to reward students for good grades and attendance during the 2007–2008 school term with Happy Meals. This had been done by Pizza Hut for a decade prior. McDonald's also initially paid to have its logo placed on the children's report cards. As noted on the Two Angry Moms website, a former agriculture secretary of Texas said that it would take two million angry moms to change the school lunch program. We really do need two million parents across America to join together against such potentially negative practices.

New York City's mayor, Michael Bloomberg, and his health commissioner, Thomas R. Frieden, provide an example of what our elected leaders, backed by a citizenry that wants to create a healthier city, can do. He has succeeded in having trans fats—by far the worse type of fat related to heart disease—removed from restaurants. Many fats are needed for health, but trans fats are not one of them. Manufactured trans fats, as opposed to the naturally occurring ones, are particularly bad for our health. Bloomberg's example is leading other cities and counties to take similar actions. And he has also focused on something that may be even more important in the long term— requiring restaurants to post the calorie content of the foods they serve. The initial legislation only required chains that already had calorie counts available to post them. This law was overturned by the courts, but has since been revised to include all chains with fifteen or more restaurants in the United States. I was asked to file the brief for the subsequent New York City court case by the state of New York. In April 2008, the courts upheld the revised law, requiring restaurants to list their calories on their menus. I'm sure the National Restaurant Association will appeal the ruling; however, with many state and local governments moving to legislate for calorie labeling, it appears that this will become mandated across the country. (King County, Washington, where Seattle is located, also requires nutrition labeling at all chain restaurants—not just those that normally post nutritional information, which turns out to be only McDonald's.)

Many other states and counties have banned trans fats, but doing so does not affect obesity. In many cases, the ban will actually lead to added fats and calories in foods. Trans fats are one type of fat, among others, that are used in the preparation of many baked and fried foods. Where there is a ban, trans fats are often replaced with an equal or greater amount of another kind of fat. When one is concerned about the number of calories consumed, the type of fat doesn't matter. Each gram of fat—be it trans fat, another saturated fat, or even canola or olive oil—contains the exact same number of calories. In contrast, listing calories on menus at restaurants might help consumers who are trying to reduce their calories, and it won't hurt those who don't care.

There are many ways that communities can become healthier by promoting physical activity and healthier eating. We should educate Americans about the need to focus on total calories more than anything else. In the end, reducing the caloric intake of all Americans—except perhaps the tiny minority of very active athletes—is critical. Our institutions can do more. Hospitals, public office buildings, and others under the jurisdiction of local governments can start to provide healthier food and beverage options in their cafeterias. Stairways can be designed as the centerpieces of new construction, as they are in many older buildings. When we walk into a building with a stairway in the front of the lobby, we tend to take the stairs. However, when stairs are closed off and are out of the way, we use the sleek escalators and elevators that are right in front of us. The same logic applies to vending machines. We can ban caloric beverages and provide water, low-fat milk, and healthier snack foods in more visible locations. Ordinances should be passed to ensure these things happen.

Encouraging our children to get involved and to take ownership in finding ways to promote healthy eating and movement is another strategy that can work. Schools and parents can help create student-run organizations much like those that oppose drinking and driving and promote safe sex. Clearly, this is an area where creative young leaders can make an impact.

It is also important to get city planners to make neighborhoods walkable and connected. Sidewalks and bike paths need to be maintained and fast traffic limited to provide safe biking. The "new urbanism" movement is focused on creating neighborhoods similar to those in Europe—communities that are walkable to both jobs and housing. If you go to any city in the Netherlands, France, or England, you'll see a lot more people walking. In Amsterdam, Vienna, and many other cities, you'll find bike paths everywhere. These principles should drive the planning of all new developments, particularly across the Sun Belt in the United States, where the population continues to climb and where the weather makes walkable communities possible. However, simply creating a new community isn't enough. Behavior has to change, too. One study showed that in a new urbanist community adults seemed to substitute walking and biking for other daily physical activity. They did little else to increase their overall activity pattern. However, this was a small study—more research is needed on all the healthy living initiatives under way.

Interestingly, France has been one of the leaders in attempting to get towns to take systematic action. In January 2004, the French began a program called EPODE (Ensemble, Prévenons l'Obésité des Enfants, or Together, Let's Prevent Obesity in Children), which targets children from five to twelve years old. Under this program, children are weighed and their BMI calculated annually. A letter explaining the results is sent to parents. Local doctors support the programs with lectures on healthy eating for parents, and dieticians visit schools. Now the program is run in more than one hundred towns, each of which also works up a series of local initiatives in grocery stores and schools and across the community to back EPODE's objectives. Schools and day care centers organize campaigns around healthy eating. Some communities have put posters and information leaflets in shops, medical centers, pharmacies, and schools. Others have community walking days and weeks, have created playgrounds with games painted on the ground, and taught kids to plant vegetables, among other activities.

Our politicians, planners, and policymakers also need to ask hard questions about what they can do to encourage healthier eating. Do we restrict fast-food restaurants so that they serve only smaller portion sizes or change pricing policy to discourage purchases of larger portion sizes? Do we encourage the more healthful, slower-fast-food restaurants to expand—such as Panera Bread, Chipotle, and Qdoba—as well as the many others that offer soups, salads, and lower-fat burritos? There is discussion in Europe about finding regulatory ways to restrict portion sizes and portion-size pricing. Portion-size pricing is the concept whereby restaurants make it cheaper for us to buy combination meals and larger portions (on a per calorie basis) than to purchase smaller portions. In many cases, it's much more expensive at fast-food restaurants to buy small drinks and sandwiches separately than large drinks and higher-calorie sandwiches in combination. From a purely practical and legal standpoint, it's unclear if this can be done in the United States.

One thing is clear. We need to find ways, in all our communities, to make supermarkets as accessible to those with lower incomes as they are to those with higher ones. Large sections of our cities are often what we call "food deserts"—inner-city areas where cheap, nutritious food is virtually unobtainable. These areas have stores or convenience stores that don't stock most types of fresh fruits and vegetables. In addition, research shows that the poor pay more for food of poorer quality. We also need to find ways to bring farmers' markets into lower-income neighborhoods, something we've had little success in doing so far. Farmers' markets and the global slow-food and organic movements are expensive and geared to upper-income pocketbooks. The slow-food movement began in Italy as a type of resistance movement to combat fast food and to preserve the cultural cuisine. A key element is the retention of heritage varieties of all foods—be they animal-source foods, such as heritage turkeys, or fruits and vegetables—and this movement is thus a close fit with the push toward eating locally and promoting farmers' markets. The slow-food, buy-local, and farmers' market movements are driven by middle- and upper-income consumers. It remains to be seen how sustainable they will be and what potential they have to benefit millions of low-income Americans. I'm skeptical that these approaches will reach the masses.

One innovative and successful effort to get healthy produce to the inner city began in seven urban neighborhoods around Schenectady and Albany, New York, that didn't have supermarkets within four miles. Several times per week a (very popular) Veggie Mobile stops near housing projects and at other fixed locations to sell fruit and vegetables that are both moderately priced and fresh. Of course, any city or state could organize such a service.

Two groups that are trying to build healthier communities are the Food Trust of Philadelphia and the North Carolina Prevention Partners. The Food Trust began in 1992 and focuses on providing access to nutritious foods in Philadelphia. In addition, it works in the schools, communities, and supermarkets; it has created farmers' markets and has even worked with corner stores to improve snack food choices. Launched by Meg Malloy, a creative public health scholar and activist, the North Carolina Prevention Partners began in 1998 to focus attention on inadequate nutrition and physical inactivity. It has worked to get insurance companies to support improved diets and increased physical activity. Insurance companies might reduce premiums for those involved in dieting and special physical activity programs, for example. It has also developed the Winner's Circle Healthy Dining Program, which works with restaurants to create healthy menu items, and it encourages hospitals to serve healthier food, among other nutrition- and inactivity-related prevention initiatives. Prevention Partners has certainly made a difference, but can only do so much without major state legislation and other support.

It helps to think about the global obesity issue in the context of the great public health advances of the past century—vaccinations, motor vehicle safety, seat belts, safer food, family planning, fluoridation of water, and reduction of tobacco use, for example.

Let's consider car seat belts. As a highway safety researcher, my wife was very involved in this issue. The Highway Safety Research Center in which she worked started promoting car seat use for infants and preschoolers long before laws were created that required them.

Infant car seats were studied to determine which were safe. Her colleagues then worked statewide to help parents install them in cars. A loaner program was created for lower-income families; a poster of my son sitting in his car seat with a seat belt around him was put in every pediatrician's office across North Carolina as part of a promotional campaign. Her center even got the American Pediatric Society to put that same poster promoting infant car seat and seat belt use into pediatricians' offices throughout America.

This team of researchers—all young adults, most of whom were parents—also did a great deal of research to learn when seat belts mattered. Their fieldwork demonstrated that an enormous number of lives were saved by the use of child car seats and seat belts. And as studies like these accumulated, governors, legislators, and advocates across the nation had more tools to use. Inexorably, advocacy turned into law. Police were also trained and educated to understand the importance of seat belt use and hence, the value of ticketing those who didn't use them.

The era of consumer activism dates back to 1965 with the publication of Ralph Nader's seminal book *Unsafe at Any Speed*, a work that promoted car safety and helped transform both the way cars are designed and tested and how drivers and passengers are protected. Nader's campaign against the automobile industry made national headlines when General Motors tried to fight him and Nader sued the automaker for some of its egregious actions in spying on him. This provided him with extensive press coverage and eventually some funds. But Nader didn't create a new era in car safety by himself. Moreover, no legislator led this charge. Public concern about child and infant deaths—and later about safety in general—did it.

Concerns about tobacco use have a similar history. In a groundbreaking British study published in 1950, researchers Sir Richard Doll and Bradford Hill showed the first link between lung cancer and smoking. The publication of the U.S. surgeon general's report on smoking in 1964 galvanized the antismoking movement in America. A year later, cigarette ads on TV were banned in the United Kingdom, and warnings were placed on such ads in the United States. Then anti-tobacco activists took advantage of something called the Fairness Doctrine. This was a Federal Communications Commission (FCC) regulation requiring broadcast licensees to present controversial topics of public importance in a manner deemed by the FCC to be honest, equitable, and balanced. It was applied in 1967 to require the tobacco industry to fund one antismoking ad for every three of its smoking ads. The initiative jump-started the reforms of 1970s. Federal cigarette taxes doubled and state taxes surged. Governments at all levels were very active in using taxation policy combined with tough advertising regulations. The figure below shows these changes and their general relationship with tobacco use. Unfortunately, the Fairness Doctrine was reversed by the Supreme Court in the 1980s.

So the anti-tobacco lobby had to face off against the global tobacco industry. Car safety advocates had to convince the automobile industry that safety was important. However, the power of the global food industry goes far beyond either of these in its scope and importance in our lives—for the simple reason that we need food to live.

Today, the drug industry dominates public expenditures and activity related to most health problems. This is as true for obesity as it is for other conditions. However, when you have such a complex disease that is caused in large part by lifestyle, it's hard to see how drugs alone will make us healthier. Changing our eating patterns is essential. But to do that we need to think big and act boldly. It's possible that we'll find a drug that will reduce our appetite or speed up our metabolism, but it's difficult to imagine that we wouldn't be healthier if we learned to be more active and eat a more balanced diet.

One way that we can change our eating pattern is through taxation policy. Taxing the added sugar in beverages is a favorite strategy of mine. It's a win-win situation. The funds from a four- or five-cents-per-gram sugar tax can fund activities that promote health and help our children. If a one-dollar can of Pepsi or Coke cost two dollars instead, we would find—as we have for cigarettes—a significant reduction in soft drink consumption. Similarly, we could tax the fat in milk to encourage consumption of reduced-fat skim and 1 percent milk. We researched some of these ideas in Mexico and found a very high responsivity to tax increases in terms of reduction in soft drink intake. Research in the United States indicates that here, too, the added costs would shift us toward drinking healthier beverages. No child after infancy will be hurt by drinking more skim milk, 1 percent milk, or water.

The consumption of fruit juice is a more complex issue. Most well-respected nutrition researchers have stated that we should drink at most four ounces of fruit juice a day. There are some mild benefits from fruit juice when consumed in limited amounts. We need to focus on educating parents and teachers about the fact that fruit juice is not helpful to a child. Even when there is no added sugar, fruit juice contains as many calories as a soft drink. Sugar is sugar, and juices have it.

We know from long experience that cigarette taxes worked to reduce tobacco use. Teens, in particular, are very sensitive to the price of cigarettes. A 10 percent price increase reduced teen smoking by 7 percent. Taxation policy doesn't require major changes in knowledge, education, or attitudes. It was one of the few things done to address tobacco cessation that could be implemented independently of other education and regulatory activities. The effectiveness of price increases also holds true for alcohol. A so-called "fat tax" would thus be another in the long line of U.S. "sin taxes."

One of the big unknowns related to taxing sugar added to

beverages is that it might encourage the consumption of diet beverages. Since we really don't know if diet beverages have negative effects on health, there's no basis to stop a tax on added sugar in beverages. I'm hopeful that over the next three to five years the research will be under way to figure out whether the consumption of diet sweeteners gets us to eat more sweets in general. But without that, and with absolutely no evidence that the long-term intake of the noncaloric sweeteners harms us, there is no basis for trying to stop increased diet soda intake. I should add the caveat that there is research that suggests some people use the fact that they are drinking a diet beverage as a rationalization for eating a lot more food, which actually increases their total calories. But I wouldn't expect this to occur on a large scale if tax policy caused some to substitute diet beverages for caloric beverages.

Scholars have recently shown that price changes will affect food choices. My research in China shows that if we tax vegetable oils, people will reduce their intake of these fats and partially replace them with increased consumption of rice, flour, soybean products, and other foods. Essentially, we've found that the reduced consumption of a vegetable oil was linked with reduced intake of fat and increased protein and carbohydrate intake. Total calories declined. Now, there are reasons why this might not be a wise intervention option—some fats are necessary, and replacing fats with refined carbohydrates and other foods may have an adverse health effect, for example—but these results do show that we need more research to understand whether taxation will improve our dietary pattern as well as reduce calorie intake. The bottom line is that we need to start making changes that will encourage us to cease consuming foods with minimal benefits and that will create revenue for our nation to begin addressing obesity.

In today's fiscal climate, major government initiatives in public health don't seem possible in many countries—particularly in the United States. Taxation policy may in fact be our best chance of generating the seed money for public health programs aimed at reducing the consumption of foods and beverages that are linked with weight gain. If we still had the Fairness Doctrine, and if public health advocates successfully applied this to the billions of dollars that the food and beverage industries spend on advertising, a great deal of money would be available for counteradvertising, research, and other activities that promote healthier diets. But it's twenty years since the repeal of the Fairness Doctrine. The reality is that we need some source of funding to initiate large-scale research and action on obesity problems in the United States and across the world. Taxation is one possible source of revenues.

Beyond caloric beverages, there is clear evidence of the effect of fast food on weight gain. However, the regulation of fast food is a complicated issue, as there are both healthy and unhealthy fast foods. Moreover, a large proportion of the United States relies on fast food. At this point, we don't know what can be done without designing huge experiments. For instance, states or counties might test options for restricting the sale of larger portions at cheaper prices. Or we might increase the price of cheese when it's added to burgers and pizza. Or we might tax fried food. Realistically, though, at this time this isn't feasible in the United States. Few countries overseas are ready for such action, either. As we've seen, it's likely that when McDonald's voluntarily introduces reduced portions or provides other healthy food options, Hardee's, Burger King, Wendy's, and others will attempt to do the opposite. Thus, regulations and legislation are needed to provide a level playing field that requires all of these companies to make the same healthy changes.

Many other foods are certainly linked with poor health, perhaps none more directly than saturated fat. While trans fats are the most pernicious of the saturated fats, all saturated fat is linked with adverse health effects. Foods that contain a high proportion of saturated fat include butter, ghee, suet, tallow, lard, coconut oil, cottonseed oil, palm kernel oil, dairy products (especially cream and cheese), meat, chocolate, and some prepared foods. Some people suggest that we tax saturated fats, but this can be a confusing issue when it comes to obesity. While most scientists acknowledge that saturated fats do affect heart disease, there are meat-rich diets, such as the Atkins plan, that have been linked with weight loss despite the high content of saturated fat in the foods consumed.

We can also use price and taxation policy to reduce the production costs of healthy food by allowing tax write-offs for some production-related expenses or by subsidizing some of the costs directly. We could do this, for example, for producers of fruits and vegetables in the same way that we subsidized livestock producers—by subsidizing credit and providing funding for price support. We could also directly or indirectly subsidize those who produce whole grains, don't over-mill grains, or significantly reduce the sugar levels in their products. For example, if Coca-Cola reduced the total sugar and calories in its products in the United States, its taxes might be lowered. Although this would be terribly difficult to work out—it would be difficult to determine how benefits would be awarded—it's still an option worth considering. We have long subsidized farmers. Why not use similar incentives to promote corporate responsibility?

Another way we can make dramatic changes in our consumption patterns is by banning advertisements in all locales and medias that reach children. We would start with banning the advertising of foods and beverages on TV before nine p.m., and we'd regulate marketing to children on all other media. As recent studies show, almost all TV food advertisements seen by American children are for products of poor nutritional quality. In addition, such a ban would extend to the placement of sweets and energy-dense snacks and drinks near check-out counters and at children's eye levels.

In the 1970s, the Federal Trade Commission proposed a rule banning or severely restricting all TV advertising to children. After years of effort, however, food lobbyists convinced Congress to amend that rule by passing the Federal Trade Commission Improvements Act of 1980. The "improvements" stripped the agency of the authority to restrict advertising. More recently, the pendulum has begun to swing the other way. Congress is again involved; Edward Markey, the chair of the House Telecommunications and Internet Subcommittee, has asked Coke, Pepsi, Unilever, General Mills, Kraft, and other major food companies to restrict their marketing of snack foods and other items. Similarly, pressure from the Federal Communications Commission, senators, and others has pressed other food companies to voluntarily limit marketing to children.

The third very clear area for reform is labeling and claims. We've all heard about products that will work wonders, such as helping us to lose twenty, forty, or more pounds. We would require independent testing and evaluation of these claims—paid for by the claimants. Similarly, independent testing would be necessary for the thousands of food items—often containing some "new" ingredient—that claim to have health benefits such as reducing heart disease, preventing cancer, or boosting weight loss. Without proof that they have the power to make us healthier, none of these products would be permitted to reach the market.

Labeling has other critical dimensions. We can also require, on the national level, that all chain restaurants label their foods with nutritional information. But we also need to study ways to improve upon current labeling methods. Currently, it can be difficult to know how many calories are in a container, as labels indicate serving size, number of servings per container, and so on. We need simpler ways to reveal not only total calories (when this is relevant), but also to educate consumers about how to read the labels. General Mills and Kellogg's are placing the total calories in a box of cereal on the front of their packages. This is one way. This would be particularly important for beverages and snack foods that are sold in larger portion sizes but that are really intended for eating at one sitting. Knowing that they would consume 220 calories by drinking a sixteen-ounce soft drink or 540 calories by eating a 110-gram chocolate bar might compel some people to reconsider what they're planning to do.

As we know, regulations limited smoking advertisements targeted at adolescents and younger children, limited cigarette sales near schools, stopped TV advertising, and in many other ways limited the ability of tobacco companies to promote their products. To some extent these have worked, but economic methods, such as taxation, seem to have had a stronger impact. Nonetheless, most scientists working to reduce smoking feel that it's the total package of taxes, regulations, and education that has been so effective.

Personally, I like the Guiding Stars program used by the Delhaize company in the United States, which I described in Chapter 6. I would love to see a global Guiding Stars initiative that would be accepted by all the major food chains as well as food companies. Such a program would be designed by scientists to encourage healthier, lower-calorie products with more whole grains, healthy fats, reduced sodium, and reduced added sugar. Kraft, Unilever, and others are working toward nationally implementing something like this for the major packaged food companies. It's important that their system be science-driven—that is, dictated by scientists and not corporate interests. I am involved in discussions to help initiate such efforts in China and Mexico.

Another major area that should be more fully explored is tort liability. There is a great potential to make meaningful changes by going after the false claims and deceptive practices of those who make and market unproven weight-loss drugs. We have no federal laws that limit companies to only making claims that are supported by randomized controlled trials. Of course, claims about certain foods being heart healthy, or beneficial in some other way, are unproven. In few cases, science backs up the claims. New federal regulations and laws would help. It's unclear how far legal action can go without new legislation.

Clearly, as we saw in previous chapters, there are many other potential courses of action. One is the removal of subsidies that promote increased intake of animal-source foods, corn, and soybeans. While soybeans themselves are good for you, consuming livestock fed with either soybeans or corn creates a less healthful option. And when we subsidize these crops, we cheapen the cost of livestock relative to the costs of fruits and vegetables. Better that we begin to find ways to increase subsidies for fruits, vegetables, and other healthy fare. Another course of action is public education. People are always in favor of this, but our efforts usually aren't effective, because we lack the will to spend the billions of dollars required to counteract Big Food and Big Beverage. For instance, the Centers for Disease Control developed a TV marketing campaign aimed at teens that promoted healthy eating and activity. Called VERB, this campaign ran from 2002 to 2006. However, Congress didn't renew the small amount of funding needed for the CDC to continue the program, despite its apparent success. Most of the $339 million spent for VERB was devoted to advertising. At the same time, Pepsi and others were spending billions on their ads.

It's hard to imagine how a public education program can have an impact in the current climate of 24/7 food and beverage advertising. Even the best, most creative, large-scale education programs won't work unless we change the broader environment in which inactivity and eating are promoted just about everywhere. As in the cigarette smoking prevention campaign, it's critical for the public to understand the harmful effects of obesity on morbidity, disability, and overall functioning. Education about the costs and effects of smoking was essential for not only the development of regulations and taxation, but also for tort liability. With regard to tobacco, it's clear that the huge class action suits with their large jury awards and monetary damages were very effective. Money always talks loudest—this is when the corporations really feel the pain. Of course, it remains to be seen if the deceptive practices of Big Tobacco are being followed by Big Food. Nevertheless, at the very least, finding ways to reduce the cacophony of food and beverage marketing and promotion is critical if we are to attain a more sensible diet.

Teaching key community leaders that have influence with parents and children—including those in the medical profession—is important. Surprisingly, few doctors understand how to discuss diet, physical activity, and a healthy lifestyle with their patients. Most pediatricians fail to tell parents that their kids are in trouble, they rarely discuss ways to change a child's diet or increase his activity, and, frankly, don't know what to do when they face overweight kids. Among government officials and researchers there is a lot of concern about the need to enlist physicians, particularly pediatricians, in the fight against obesity. The National Institutes of Health has funded a number of studies to create approaches to do this, and several of my colleagues have been working on improving ways to educate doctors. Their approach has been to create simple materials—such as forms that walk the doctor and patient through a guide to a healthier diet—that can be quickly implemented. Doctors need education and materials that will help them ease their patients into healthier lifestyles. Much more work needs to be done on this across all medical professions that deal with the public.

Economists—and many others—worry about whether we should

interfere with the rights of individuals. They note we had a strong rationale for intervention with smoking because cigarette use passively affects nonsmokers. However, we didn't know much about the effects of secondhand smoke until the 1980s. In fact, the 1982 surgeon general's report on smoking and cancer reviewed the first three epidemiological studies on the relationship between passive smoking and lung cancer. The evidence was limited and the reports' conclusions were quite tentative. So, how did we justify antismoking interventions at the state and national levels a decade or two earlier? The answer: the large health costs involved and the clear linkage of smoking with disease.

Of course, there will never be as clear a case for any one food causing obesity and diabetes as there was for cigarette smoking causing lung cancer. Also, obesity isn't an infectious disease that spreads from one person to another. We require that all children attending school be vaccinated against a number of common diseases, but, obviously, this isn't an option for obesity. As discussed in Chapter 5, however, there is a lot of evidence that the health costs of obesity in terms of increased morbidity, hospitalization, earlier use of retirement homes, and increased disability far outweigh those of smoking. Obesity debilitates; it does not kill quickly. This means that we can linger for decades in poor health, requiring extensive medical care and medication.

So, how realistic are my recommendations? Recognition of the importance of obesity and the need for action is beginning to show up in public opinion around the world. As my state legislator told me, promoting laws related to child obesity is very popular at the moment. Actions such as taxing soft drinks, which are unthinkable today, will become doable in three to five years. No one would ever have believed that smoking could be barred from restaurants, or that restaurants would be required to eliminate the use of trans fats. Time, persistence, and, most of all, a bold vision of a better, healthier future are necessary for a successful outcome. In Mexico for instance, after much effort, we've seen huge changes in their poverty and welfare programs and I expect major shifts in regulations and taxation policies to follow. The Mexican government is desperate and the congress, the secretary of health, and others recognize the critical nature of their country's problem. When this same feeling of desperation begins to appear in other countries, we'll see action. And success will beget success. We need examples that work. I'm hopeful that Mexico will be one such example.

Rather than get better, the crisis will accelerate. Parents who today think that all that is needed are restrictions for vending machines in the schools will find that their teens have diabetes. Only harsher actions taken now can reverse this trend. Will public opinion change fast enough? Will big industry counterattack in ways that weaken stronger legislation? These are issues that only time will tell about.

At the global level, an essential first step is a consensus that poor dietary and physical activity patterns and obesity are critical public health problems of all nations—rich and poor. Fortunately, this action was taken by the World Health Organization (WHO) and its assembly of member nations in 2004 following several expert committee reports by the World Health Organization and the Food and Agriculture Organization of the United Nations (WHO/FAO). The food industry objected to many of the issues raised in these documents, particularly in regard to sugar. However, the WHO board, and subsequently its member nations, refused to buckle to pressure and voted in a major show of consensus that, like HIV/AIDS, poor dietary and activity patterns and obesity were indeed a global pandemic. In fact, the two major WHO decrees of the past decade dealt with these two global health problems. The WHO global strategy on diet, physical activity, and health focused on many of the concerns discussed in this book: added sugar, energy-dense food, and reduced physical activity.

Actions taken by the World Health Organization don't lead to immediate action, but they do help. They are a first step. An important second step is to get the institutions that are supporting the developing world's growth to include the global obesity pandemic as part of their funding considerations. This means getting the World Bank, the Asian Development Bank, the Interamerican Bank, the European Bank for Reconstruction and Development, and the African Development Bank to shift programs, policies, and major loans. However, these international agencies have concentrated on promoting the production of sugarcane, sugar beets, livestock, and basic grains. They'll acknowledge that global obesity is a concern, but the World Bank and the other regional finance organizations haven't moved beyond poverty and micronutrient deficiencies to examine the broader health needs of many countries in which they are working. As leaders not only in making loans and grants, but also of policy work that spearheads the development and planning of many nations, this is a sad situation.

Today, when the World Bank and regional banks consider the needs of the Americas, Asia, and the Middle East, they focus on malnutrition. The lapse is striking. In its own documents dating back to 1990, major voices in the World Bank identified chronic diseases as the central health problems of Brazil and China. Yet the health programs and policies of the World Bank ignored these concerns. Even more important, World Bank agricultural loans and grants didn't take chronic diseases into account. Because much of the developing world has conquered hunger, there is now a need for these countries to turn their attention to obesity and nutrition-related noncommunicable diseases. Besides international agencies, bilateral agencies such as the U.S. Agency for International Development and its counterparts in Europe and Japan have done little to change their focus toward obesity. Of course, we still have seven hundred million hungry people in the world. But we also must prepare for the future—and for much of the world, the future is now.

While the United States has not yet faced the obesity problem on a national level, a number of countries have. Brazil is one of the leaders in this area. Brazil requires that 70 percent of all food purchased by schools come from local areas, with a focus on fruits, vegetables, and other healthy items. This was done to reduce processed food intake. As we've seen, Mexico's Ministry of Health is very concerned about the explosion in child and adult obesity and has made caloric sweetened beverages one of its first targets. Poverty programs across Mexico, which serve more than ten million people, have switched from whole milk to 1.5 percent reduced-fat milk, and they plan to move to skim milk within a year. And if the taxation initiatives that we're expecting to become law in Mexico are effective, this will be an important example for other countries to follow.

In the Middle East and Africa, despite the great need for serious change, only Mauritania seems to be taking real action. After a 2001 national survey found that more than 40 percent of its female population was overweight, the government instituted sweeping innovations. Using television commercials, radio and TV skits, physician support, and other approaches, they've succeeded in slowly turning a culture that prized Rubenesque women to exercise and eat right. It's a long, slow process, but they're getting women moving and concerned. And they are getting some men to see that it's better for their wives and daughters to carry a healthy weight.

What Can We Do?

As expected, the Scandinavian countries are far ahead of the rest of the world. Sweden banned food and beverage advertising aimed at children in 1991; then they strengthened the law in 1996. Elsewhere in Europe, the countries with the worst problems—Spain, Italy, and England—have done little to date.

South Korea has done the most between 1970 and 2000 to hold back the vast changes in diet that other rapidly developing economies are experiencing. South Korea systematically trained new house-wives to cook the traditional low-fat, healthy vegetable dishes that are important to the country's classical cuisine. At the same time, the government encouraged the continued consumption of the tradi-tional cuisine with advertising campaigns. For a country with South Korea's level of development, the result was a national diet whose proportion of energy from fat was far below what one would expect, one of the highest vegetable intake levels in the world, and one-third the obesity rate of countries with similar economies. Nonetheless, in recent years, global economic treaties that promote free trade across the world along with other factors yet to be fully understood, such as the impact of movies and television, have led to a rapid shift in South Korea away from healthful eating to a less desirable path of increas-ing fast-food intake and rapidly declining vegetable consumption.

A compelling model of how change can result from crisis comes, unlikely enough, from Cuba. The economic decline that followed the collapse of the Soviet Union put an end to food subsidies to Cuba, its access to cheap Soviet oil, and Soviet purchases of Cuban sugar. The economic collapse that resulted in Cuba was rapid and dramatic. The Cuban economic crises from 1989 to 2000 led to significant gasoline shortages and rapid increases in food prices. However, this resulted in reductions in energy intake as people ate less, an increase in physi-cal activity as people walked more, and, consequently, in large reduc-tions in both weight and obesity. Deaths from diabetes, linked both with obesity and inactivity, declined by half. Deaths from heart disease and stroke also declined.

I'm hopeful that the rapid changes in a few countries toward more aggressively addressing overeating will lead to some successful efforts in the next few years. Other countries will then jump on the bandwagon. I have high hopes for Mexico, which could become a world leader in this area. The major changes planned by the Mexican government—in taxation, subsidy policy, and other areas—will first change the society's beverage pattern and later push the population toward a healthier diet. Mexico will be modeling important work for the rest of us. France and other countries are trying with projects such as the French EPODE program, but the results for large populations remain to be evaluated. Many countries are floundering; they're focusing on narrow issues such as trying to fund community education programs. I think that this is missing the big picture. In the seat-belt use and antismoking campaigns, regulations and taxation were critical. And as we've seen, the food industry initially tried to blame reduced physical activity—rather than its own products and machinations—for the problem. We have to recognize that excessive caloric intake is a major problem, and we must find ways to cut calories. Yes, some food companies are beginning to try to take actions, as I've noted. But while there are some positive forces for change in the food industry, most are doing business as usual—just as Big Tobacco did for so many decades.

In retrospect, this book is a tale of two worlds. The first is the world of the global food industry and the global medical industry, both of which gain far more from living with the obesity problem than from curing it. The second world is the one slowly emerging. It is complicated yet visionary. It is a world united in its resolve to prevent these problems by first understanding their underlying causes and then by creating macroeconomic and political solutions. Right now, the former world is winning completely. But there are genuine signs of hope in many countries that ought to inspire us. I even see some kernels of hope within the global food industry.

The world has become fat in just a few decades. The changes in how we eat, drink, and move that have affected billions of people over the last half-century will affect billions more in the coming years. If we don't do something to stop and reverse these changes, in a few thousand years the only survivors may be those in our species who don't store fat, who hate sweet foods and love activity. In just a short period we will be turning evolution on its head, undoing a process that has taken hundreds of thousands of years to get us to where we are today. Or perhaps we'll permanently split into two worlds—one where the wealthy pop pills to deal with the health consequences of our bad choices, and a second world where the poor will be fat and have terrible health problems.

I hope we choose the path of prevention and health. I hope we come together to seek larger-scale solutions to address the ever-growing and seemingly intractable problems of our own making.

ACKNOWLEDGMENTS

I became a scholar soon after I stopped being a social activist. In both roles, my focus has been on poverty and hunger in the world, but I never thought my career would take me in the directions it has. I certainly never thought I would write a book about how we eat, drink, and move as these relate to obesity and other issues. Nor did I ever think I would know as much as I do about the global food industry.

My scholarship grew out of an amazing experience in India during my senior year in college and a subsequent year at the University of Wisconsin–Madison. My senior honors thesis on the economics of nutrition launched me on my career as a researcher, teacher, and mentor. I owe my initial debts to those who helped me travel to India—Henry Hart and Joe Elder—and my economics professors and advisers—Ralph Andreano and Lee Hansen (all at the University of Wisconsin–Madison). They allowed me to explore nutrition economics for my thesis and led me to meet and interact with Alfred Harper, an eminent nutrition biochemist with a broad view of his field.

After being away from the university and involved in intense political and social activism, I happened to have a lucky break. I ran into an old acquaintance, Jim Levinson, who introduced me to two wonderful faculty at Cornell University—Michael Latham and David Call. They accepted me into the doctoral program they were building and hired me as a deputy director of their new International Nutrition Program. I was helped and inspired by others at Cornell, particularly Dan Sisler and Daphne Roe, with whom I had long discussions about food and nutrition and who provided me with an appreciation of history.

I gained equally from my thesis work in the Philippines and from later collaboration with Florentino and Nenita Solon (director and head of communications research, respectively, at the Nutrition Center of the Philippines)—two close colleagues and friends.

An important person in my post-Cornell scholarly life in Asia was Bob Evenson of Yale. Bob and I undertook some very intense village-level studies that helped me devise my broad-based way of looking at rural life in Asia. This has served me in great stead as I have developed and refined many household-based multipurpose surveys from the 1970s to the present.

For the past thirty years, my scholarly home has been the Carolina Population Center (CPC) of the Nutrition Department at the University of North Carolina's School of Public Health. The director of the CPC, J. Richard Udry, has been a key mentor and guide who has helped me accomplish many goals. Dick helped me bring John Akin and David Guilkey, two economists, into the CPC, and allowed me to develop with them rather unusual research on maternal and infant nutrition and health. Our work has ranged from evaluating food and nutrition programs in the U.S. to huge studies of the determinants, patterns, and consequences of infant feeding on the mother and infant in Cebu, Philippines, where Wilhelm Flieger became a central partner.

From the Cebu, Philippines, period onward, Linda Adair has been one of my key collaborators. She has provided advice and assistance at many junctures. Her ability to integrate biological and behavioral relationships and her comradeship have been most important to my development.

When I initiated research in China, I began to pull back and study the broad history of dietary change in the world, and I realized how rapidly we were starting to shift toward a world dominated by obesity. My work on this topic started with the collaboration of Gail Henderson and John Akin. The other major set of collaborators who have had the most to do with me in terms of this book and thinking are those from China. A very wise classically educated scholar and nutritionist, Chen Chunming, shared my vision for the China survey work. I also worked very closely and have had wonderful collaborations with Ge Keyou, Du Shufa, and Zhai Fengying.

As I moved into the obesity arena and built my new scholarly life, several major scholars influenced and assisted me. Steve Zeisel in my Department of Nutrition unleashed the last two decades of great productivity for me. He allowed me not only to build with him in the nutrition department but also to build the Nutrition Epidemiology Program and to hire numerous wonderful colleagues.

I began my work on the nutrition transition research with another great scholar, Carlos Monteiro of Brazil. He and I have written dozens of papers together, and his work has been influential on my thinking. Two more colleagues have encouraged me, worked with me, and helped me over the past two decades—Tim Lang and Geoffrey Cannon.

In the mid-1990s, I was joined by Penny Gordon-Larsen, another nutrition collaborator who has worked closely with me on several large-scale initiatives in the United States and now on international work. Anna Maria Siega-Riz and Pam Haines are two other colleagues with whom I have worked extensively, and I thank them.

Acknowledgments

Senior leaders I have worked with and continue to work with include George Bray of Pennington Research Center, Walter Willett of Harvard University, and Ben Caballero of Johns Hopkins University. Ben and I prepared a book on the nutrition transition.

My postdoctoral fellows and amazing doctoral students have been very important in opening new issues, thoughts, and approaches to me. I owe them a great deal of thanks for what they have added to my life and my career. I can only hope I have helped them one-tenth as much as they helped me in building my understanding of a vast number of social and biological issues as they relate to obesity and how we eat, drink, and move. In many ways they are the inspiration that keeps me working.

Throughout all of these projects and all the personal and professional ups and downs, my right hand and administrative assistant, Frances Dancy, has been there. Her importance to me and my group of colleagues is immeasurable.

Preparation of this book has seen some other important heroes. My agent, Jill Marsal of the Sandra Dijkstra Agency, did yeoman's work in placing my book with Avery. At an early stage, Bill Shapbell helped clean up the chapters. Susan Leon was invaluable in editing and refining the book. Jeff Galas put in major work pruning and focusing the book. Tom Swasey has worked with me since the first day on graphics for all my nutrition transition presentations and with this book.

Then there is my family: my career began and will end with their great support. I grew up in a close, wonderful family. I visited my grandmother daily, saw relatives on my mother's side almost weekly, and saw most other cousins and uncles annually, if not more frequently.

My sister-in-law, Susan Shirk, gets special thanks for encouraging me to follow her footsteps and write a popular book. She introduced me to my agent and suggested my book title. Another family member, Carla Cohen, also encouraged me over the years to write this book.

My brother Sam, sister Merle, brother-in-law Bernie Wexler, and all my nieces and nephews (David, Devra, Lucy, and Tamara) have been equally supportive. Most important is my son, Matt, who has put up with my work and projects over the years.

I dedicate the book to my son, and to my departed partner, Anne-Linda Furstenberg, whom I miss very much. I wish Anne-Linda were here to share in these joys.

I also want to dedicate this book to my extended family, for whom food remains a major component of life. My love of good food and drink comes from them.

SOURCES AND REFERENCES

The following are some of the many articles and books that I have consulted in writing this book and that have influenced my point of view. Because I wrote this book for the general reader, this list is perhaps not as complete as one would find in a scholarly work. Nonetheless, many of the articles listed below are written by and for specialists. For each chapter, I've noted which sources are of potential interest to nonspecialists. All of my articles that I have included are accessible to a nonspecialist. Most of the references are primary resources, except for the popular texts and books I have included.

1. A BRIEF HISTORY OF THE MODERN DIET

On the historical changes in our diet:
The most important sets of studies here are the work of Eaton, Konner, and colleagues on the Paleolithic diet; the historical work of Mintz on sugar; Roe on pellagra; Trowell and Burkitt, and Truswell and Hansen on the Westernization of our diet. The Corn, Eaton et al., and Roe books are written for the nonspecialist.

Sources and References

Brezhnev, Leonid Il'ich. 1967. The report of the General Secretary of the Central Committee of the Communist Party of the Soviet Union. In *The Proceedings of the XXIV Congress of the CPSU*. Moscow: Russian Central Committee (Gospolitizdat).

An interesting historical document on the push in the former Soviet Union to promote meat.

Corn, Charles. 1998. *The Scents of Eden. A History of the Spice Trade*. New York, Tokyo, London. Kodansha International.

Dillehay, Tom D., Jack Rossen, Thomas C. Andres, and David E. Williams. 2007. Preceramic adoption of peanut, squash, and cotton in northern Peru. *Science* 316 (5833):1890–93.

Eaton, S. Boyd, Stanley Boyd Eaton, 3rd, and M. J. Konner. 1997. Paleolithic nutrition revisited: a twelve-year retrospective on its nature and implications. *European Journal of Clinical Nutrition* 51 (4):207–16.

Eaton, S. Boyd, and M. Konner. 1985. Paleolithic nutrition: A consideration on its nature and current implications. *New England Journal of Medicine* 312:283–9.

Eaton, S. Boyd, M. Shostak, and M. Konner. 1988. *The Paleolithic Prescription: A Program of Diet and Exercise and a Design for Living*. New York: Harper & Row.

Harris, David. 1981. The prehistory of human subsistence: a speculative outline. In *Food, Nutrition and Evolution: Food as an Environmental Factor in the Genesis of Human Variability*, ed. D. N. Walcher and N. N. Kretchmer. New York: Masson.

Jönsson, Tommy, Bo Ahren, Giovanni Pacini, Frank Sundler, Nils Wierup, Stig Steen, Trygve Sjöberg, Martin Ugander, Johan Frostegård, Leif Göransson, and Staffan Lindeberg. 2006. A Paleolithic diet confers higher insulin sensitivity, lower C-reactive protein and lower blood pressure than a cereal-based diet in domestic pigs. *Nutrition & Metabolism* 3:39.

Milton, Giles. 2000. *Nathaniel's Nutmeg: Or the True and Incredible Adventures of the Spice Trader Who Changed the Course of History*. New York: Penguin.

Mintz, Sidney. 1986. *Sweetness and Power: The Place of Sugar in Modern History*. New York: Penguin.

Mintz, Sidney W. 1979. Time, sugar and sweetness. *Marxist Perspectives* 2 (4):56–73.

Moll-Weiss, Augusta. 1910. *Le foyer domestique: Cours d'économie domestique, d'hygiène et de cuisine pratique professé à l'École des Mères de Bordeaux*. Paris: Hachette.

Moll-Weiss, Augusta. 1930. De la meilleure utilisation du salaire familial. *L'Art Ménager* 42:261.

The person I credit with beginning portion control in France and the person whose writing and work built this into a national program.

Roe, Daphne. 1973. *A Plague of Corn: The Social History of Pellagra*. Ithaca, New York: Cornell University Press.

Schwartz, Stuart B. 2004. *Tropical Babylons: Sugar and the Making of the Atlantic World, 1450–1680*. Chapel Hill: University of North Carolina Press.

Steckel, Richard H. and Jerome C. Rose, ed. 2002. *The Backbone of History: Health and Nutrition in the Western Hemishpere*. Cambridge, UK: Cambridge University Press.

Trowell, H. C., and D. P. Burkitt, eds. 1981. *Western Diseases: Their Emergence and Prevention*. Cambridge, MA: Harvard University Press.

Truswell, A. S. 1977. Diet and nutrition of hunter-gathers. In *Health and Diseases in Tribal Societies*, Ciba Foundation Symposium 49. Amsterdam: Elsevier.

Truswell, A. S., and J. D. L. Hansen. 1976. Medical research among the !Kung. In *Kalahari Hunter-gatherers: Studies of the !Kung San and Their Neighbors*, ed. R. B. Lee and I. DeVore. Cambridge, MA: Harvard University Press.

On the dietary and food composition trends in the United States and around the globe in the last half-century:

Davis, Donald R., Melvin D. Epp, and Hugh D. Riordan. 2004. Changes in USDA food composition data for 43 garden crops, 1950 to 1999. *Journal of the American College of Nutrition* 23 (6):669–82.

Delgado, Christopher L. 2003. Rising consumption of meat and milk in developing countries has created a new food revolution. *Journal of Nutrition* 133 (11 Suppl 2):3907S–3910S.

Delgado, Christopher L., Mark W. Rosegrant, and S. Meijer. 2001. Livestock to 2020: The Revolution Continues. Paper presented at the annual meetings of the International Agricultural Trade Research Consortium (IATRC), 18–19 January, at Auckland, New Zealand.

Duffey, Kiyah, and Barry M. Popkin. In press. High-fructose corn syrup: Is this what's for dinner? *American Journal of Clinical Nutrition.*

Duffey, Kiyah, and Barry M. Popkin. 2007. Shifts in patterns and consumption of beverages between 1965 and 2002. *Obesity* 15 (11):2739–47.

Haines, Pamela S., Mary Y. Hama, David K. Guilkey, and Barry M. Popkin. 2003. Weekend eating in the United States is linked with greater energy, fat, and alcohol intake. *Obesity Research* 11 (8):945–9.

Jahns, Lisa, Anna Maria Siega-Riz, and Barry M. Popkin. 2001. The increasing prevalence of snacking among U.S. children from 1977 to 1996. *Journal of Pediatrics* 138 (4):493–8.

Mayer, Anne-Marie. 1997. Historical changes in the mineral content of fruits and vegetables. *British Food Journal* 99:207–11.

Nielsen, Samara J., and Barry M. Popkin. 2003. Patterns and trends in food portion sizes, 1977-1998. *Journal of the American Medical Association* 289 (4):450–3.

Nielsen, Samara J., Anna Maria Siega-Riz, and Barry M. Popkin. 2002. Trends in energy intake in U.S. between 1977 and 1996: similar shifts seen across age groups. *Obesity Research* 10 (5):370–8.

———. 2002. Trends in food locations and sources among adolescents and young adults. *Preventive Medicine* 35 (2):107–13.

Peck, Gregory M., Preston K. Andrews, John P. Reganold, and John K. Fellman. 2006. Apple orchard productivity and fruit quality under organic, conventional, and integrated management. *HortScience* 41:99–107.

Popkin, Barry M., Alexander Baturin, Lenore Kohlmeier, and Namvar Zohoori. 1997. Russia: monitoring nutritional change during the reform period. In *Implementing Dietary Guidelines for Healthy Eating,* ed. V. Wheelock. London: Chapman and Hall.

Rozin, Paul, Kimberly Kabnick, Erin Pete, Claude Fischler, and Christy Shields. 2003. The ecology of eating: smaller portion sizes in France than in the United States help explain the French paradox. *Psychological Science* 14 (5):450–54.

Wansink, Brian. 2004. Environmental factors that increase the food intake and consumption volume of unknowing consumers. *Annual Review of Nutrition* 24:455–79.

———. 2006. What really determines what we eat. The hidden truth. *Diabetes Self-Management* 23 (6):44, 47–8, 51.

———. 2006. *Mindless Eating: Why We Eat More Than We Think.* New York: Bantam-Dell.

Wansink, Brian, and Matthew M. Cheney. 2005. Super Bowls: serving bowl size and food consumption. *Journal of the American Medical Association* 293 (14):1727–8.

Wansink, Brian, James E. Painter, and Jill North. 2005. Bottomless bowls: why visual cues of portion size may influence intake. *Obesity Research* 13 (1):93–100.

Watson, James L., ed. 1997. *Golden Arches East: McDonald's in East Asia.* Stanford, CA: Stanford University Press.

One of the few case studies to go in-depth across many countries into the role of the modern food sector, in this case McDonald's, on eating behaviors.

Winter, Carl K., and Sarah F. Davis. 2006. Organic foods. *Journal of Food Science* 71 (9):R117--R124.

Young, L.R., and M. Nestle 2003. Expanding portion sizes in the U.S. marketplace: implications for nutrition counseling. *Journal of the American Dietetic Association* 103 (2):231–4.

Young, L.R., and M.S. Nestle. 1995. Portion sizes in dietary assessment: issues and policy implications. *Nutrition Reviews* 53(6): 149–58.

Zizza, Claire, Anna Maria Siega-Riz, and Barry M. Popkin. 2001. Significant increase in young adults' snacking between 1977–1978 and 1994–1996 represents a cause for concern! *Preventive Medicine* 32 (4):303–10.

On diet, obesity, and health:

The Willett book is written for the nonspecialist.

Bjelakovic, Goran, Dimitrinka Nikolova, Lise Lotte Gluud, Rosa G. Simonetti, and Christian Gluud. 2007. Mortality in randomized trials of antioxidant supplements for primary and secondary prevention: systematic review and meta-analysis. *Journal of the American Medical Association* 297 (8):842–57.

Sources and References

Bray, George A., and Barry M. Popkin. 1998. Dietary fat intake does affect
obesity! *American Journal of Clinical Nutrition* 68 (6):1157–73.
A coherent argument for the reasons why a high-fat diet will affect weight
gain. Subsequent clinical studies show that a reduced-fat diet will lead to
reduced weight as will a low-carbohydrate diet.

Burkitt, Denis P. 1973. Some diseases characteristic of modern Western
civilization. *British Medical Journal* 1 (5848):274–8.

———. 1973. Some diseases characteristic of modern Western civilization.
A possible common causative factor. *Clinical Radiology* 24 (3):271–80.

Caballero, Benjamin. 2008. Food to die for? *British Medical Journal* 336
(7646):723.

Ding, Eric L., Susan M. Hutfless, Xin Ding, and Saket Girotra. 2006.
Chocolate and prevention of cardiovascular disease: a systematic review.
Nutrition & Metabolism 3:2.

Gardner, Christopher D., Alexandre Kiazand, Sofiya Alhassan, Soowon Kim,
Randall S. Stafford, Raymond R. Balise, Helena C. Kraemer, and Abby C.
King. 2007. Comparison of the Atkins, Zone, Ornish, and LEARN diets for
change in weight and related risk factors among overweight premenopausal
women: the A-to-Z Weight Loss Study: a randomized trial. *Journal of the
American Medical Association* 297 (9):969–77.
One of the best of all the studies examining the effects of various dietary
plans on weight loss and health over an eleven-month period.

Hermann, F., L. E. Spieker, F. Ruschitzka, I. Sudano, M. Hermann, C.
Binggeli, T. F. Luscher, W. Riesen, G. Noll, and R. Corti. 2006. Dark
chocolate improves endothelial and platelet function. *Heart* 92 (1):119–20.

Kral, Tanja V. E., and Barbara J. Rolls. 2004. Energy density and portion size:
their independent and combined effects on energy intake. *Physiology &
Behavior* 82 (1):131–8.

Mancini, M., and J. Stamler. 2004. Diet for preventing cardiovascular diseases:
light from Ancel Keys, distinguished centenarian scientist. *Nutrition,
Metabolism & Cardiovascular Diseases* 14 (1):52–7.

Mursu, Jaakko, Sari Voutilainen, Tarja Nurmi, Tiina H. Rissanen, Jyrki K.
Virtanen, Jari Kaikkonen, Kristiina Nyyssonen, and Jukka T. Salonen. 2004.

Sources and References

Dark chocolate consumption increases HDL cholesterol concentration and chocolate fatty acids may inhibit lipid peroxidation in healthy humans. *Free Radical Biology and Medicine* 37 (9):1351–9.

Rolls, Barbara J. 2003. The supersizing of America: portion size and the obesity epidemic. *Nutrition Today* 38 (2):42–53.

Rolls, Barbara J., Erin L. Morris, and Liane S. Roe. 2002. Portion size of food affects energy intake in normal-weight and overweight men and women. *American Journal of Clinical Nutrition* 76 (6):1207–13.

Rolls, Barbara J., Liane S. Roe, T. V. Kral, J. S. Meengs, and D. E. Wall. 2004. Increasing the portion size of a packaged snack increases energy intake in men and women. *Appetite* 42 (1):63–9.

Steiner, Jacob E., Dieter Glaser, Maria E. Hawilo, and Kent C. Berridge. 2001. Comparative expression of hedonic impact: affective reactions to taste by human infants and other primates. *Neuroscience & Biobehavioral Reviews* 25 (1):53–74.

Vanitallie, Theodore B. 2005. Ancel Keys: a tribute. *Nutrition & Metabolism* 2 (1):4.

Vlachopoulos, Charalambos, Nikolaos Alexopoulos, and Christodoulos Stefanadis. 2006. Effect of dark chocolate on arterial function in healthy individuals: cocoa instead of ambrosia? *Current Hypertension Reports* 8 (3):205–11.

Willett, Walter C. 1998. Is dietary fat a major determinant of body fat? *American Journal of Clinical Nutrition* 67 (3 Suppl):556S–62S.

———. 2001. *Eat, Drink, and Be Healthy: The Harvard Medical School Guide to Healthy Eating.* New York: Simon & Schuster.

Willett, Walter C., and A. Ascherio. 1994. Trans fatty acids: are the effects only marginal? *American Journal of Public Health* 84 (5):722–4.

Walt Willet was the major scholar who single-handedly pushed the trans fatty acid issue into the consciousness of the nutrition and medical communities. He also is a strong believer in the roles of good and bad fats in our diet. He has argued that the excessive focus on fat was unhealthy.

World Health Organization. 2008. *Obesity and overweight.* WHO 2008. www.who.int/bmi/index.jsp?introPage-intro_4_3.html. Consulted April 12, 2008.

Sources and References

On sweetness:
The Yudkin book is written for the nonspecialist.

Desor, J. A., and G. K. Beauchamp. 1987. Longitudinal changes in sweet
preferences in humans. *Physiology & Behavior* 39 (5):639–41.

Yudkin, John. 1964. Dietary fat and dietary sugar in relation to ischemic heart-
disease and diabetes. *Lancet* 2:4.

———. 1972. *Sweet and Dangerous: The New Facts About the Sugar You Eat as a
Cause of Heart Disease, Diabetes, and Other Killers*. New York: David McKay.
John Yudkin was the lone voice in the scholarly world in the 1960s and 1970s
noting that the focus solely on fat was misguided and sugar in all its forms
was an equally important factor to be considered.

On U.S. agricultural policy:
Schaffer, Harwood D., Douglas B. Hunt, and Daryll E. Ray. 2007. U.S.
Agricultural Commodity Policy and Its Relationship to Obesity. In
Wingspread Conference at Racine, WI.

Starmer, Elanor, Aimee Witteman, and Timothy A. Wise. 2006. Feeding the
factory farm: implicit subsidies to the broiler chicken industry. Working
paper 06–03, Global Development and Environment Institute, Tufts
University.

Broad-based discussions of food and nutritional issues:
The Love and Pollan books are written for the nonspecialist.

Love, John F. 1995. *McDonald's: Behind the Arches*. Rev. sub. ed. New York:
Bantam.

Pollan, Michael. 2008. *In Defense of Food: An Eater's Manifesto*. New York:
Penguin Press.
Michael Pollan is the journalist who has done the most in the United States
to push the slow-food, or locavore, or eat-and-buy-local, approach. He also is
very much against processed and industrialized food and provides coherent
arguments for his approach.

2. WE ARE WHAT WE DRINK

On historical changes in how we drink:

The Cordain, Johnson, Macfarlane, and Tannahill books are written for the nonspecialist.

Atkins, Peter J. 1992. White poison? The social consequences of milk consumption, 1850–1930. *Social History of Medicine* 5 (2):207–27.

Cordain, Loren. 2002. *The Paleo Diet: Lose Weight and Get Healthy by Eating the Food You Were Designed to Eat.* Hoboken, NJ: John Wiley & Sons.

Hyams, Edward. 1965. *Dionysus: A Social History of the Wine Vine.* New York: Macmillan.

Johnson, Hugh. 1989. *Vintage: The Story of Wine.* New York: Simon & Schuster.

Kiple, Kenneth F., and Kriemhild Coneè Ornelas, eds. 2000. *The Cambridge World History of Food.* Cambridge, UK; New York: Cambridge University Press.

Lu, Yu. 1974. *The Classic of Tea.* Trans. Francis Ross Carpenter. Boston: Little, Brown.

Macfarlane, Alan, and Iris Macfarlane. 2003. *Green Gold: The Empire of Tea.* London: Ebury.

Newman, James L. 2000. III.13. Wine. In *The Cambridge World History of Food*, edited by K. F. Kiple and K. C. Ornelas. New York: Cambridge University Press.

Standage, Tom. 2005. *A History of the World in Six Glasses.* New York: Walker & Co.

Steele, James H. 2000. History, trends, and extent of pasteurization. *Journal of the American Veterinary Medical Association* 217 (2):175–8.

Swallow, Dallas M. 2003. Genetics of lactase persistence and lactose intolerance. *Annual Review of Genetics* 37:197–219.

Tannahill, Reay. 1989. *Food in History.* New, fully revised and updated edition. New York: Crown.

Tishkoff, Sarah A., Floyd A. Reed, Alessia Ranciaro, Benjamin F. Voight, Courtney C. Babbitt, Jesse S. Silverman, Kweli Powell, Holly M. Mortensen, Jibril B. Hirbo, Maha Osman, Muntaser Ibrahim, Sabah A. Omar, Godfrey

Sources and References

Lema, Thomas B. Nyambo, Jilur Ghori, Suzannah Bumpstead, Jonathan K. Pritchard, Gregory A. Wray, and Panos Deloukas. 2006. Convergent adaptation of human lactase persistence in Africa and Europe. *Nature Genetics* 39 (1):31–40.

Topik, Steven C. 2000. Coffee. In *The Cambridge World History of Food*, ed. K. F. Kiple and K. C. Ornelas. Cambridge, UK; New York: Cambridge University Press.

Weisburger, John H., and James Comer. 2000. III.11. Tea. In *The Cambridge World History of Food*, ed. K. F. Kiple and K. C. Ornelas. Cambridge, UK; New York: Cambridge University Press.

Wolf, A., G. A. Bray, and B. M. Popkin. 2008. A short history of beverages and how our body treats them. *Obesity Reviews* 9:151–64.

Some beverage industry case studies:

The Clark and Pendergrast books are written for the nonspecialist.

Anon. 2002. Red Bull's Dietrich Mateschitz. *Economist*, May 9.
   The Red Bull story is fascinating and yet to be written. It grew at record speed into a global beverage and essentially created a new genre of beverages, one which may yet threaten the public's health.

Clark, Taylor. 2007. *Starbucked: A Double Tall Tale of Caffeine, Commerce, and Culture*. New York: Little, Brown.

Coca-Cola Company website. Consulted December 18, 2006.

Dolan, Kerry A. 2005. The Soda with Buzz. *Forbes*, March 28, 126.

Pendergrast, Mark. 1999. *Uncommon Grounds: The History of Coffee and How It Transformed Our World*. New York: Basic Books.

Pendergrast, Mark. 2000. *For God, Country & Coca-Cola: The Definitive History of the Great American Soft Drink and the Company That Makes It*. New York: Basic Books.
   Pendergrast has written two quite informative books about the history of both companies. They are fairly complete balanced histories and very well written.

Sources and References

On beverage trends in the United States and around the globe in the last half-century:

Barquera, Simón, F. Campirano, A. Bonvecchio, L. Hernández, J. Espinosa, Juan Rivera, and Barry M. Popkin. 2007. Trends and characteristics of caloric beverage consumption in Mexican preschool and school-age children. Cuernavaca.

Barquera, Simón, L. Hernández, M. L. Tolentino, J. Espinosa, J. Leroy, Juan Rivera, and Barry M. Popkin. In press. Dynamics of adolescent and adult beverage intake patterns in Mexico. *Journal of Nutrition*.
These two Mexican papers document the most rapid increase in intake of caloric beverages I have seen globally. The changes documented in Mexico are unprecedented.

Carson, Terry A., Anna Maria Siega-Riz, and Barry M. Popkin. 1999. The importance of breakfast meal type to daily nutrient intake: differences by age and ethnicity. *Cereal Foods World* 44:414–22.

Duffey, Kiyah, and Barry M. Popkin. 2007. Shifts in patterns and consumption of beverages between 1965 and 2002. *Obesity* 15 (11):2739–47.

Haines, Pamela S., Mary Y. Hama, David K. Guilkey, and Barry M. Popkin. 2003. Weekend eating in the United States is linked with greater energy, fat, and alcohol intake. *Obesity Research* 11 (8):945–9.

Nielsen, Samara J., Anna Maria Siega-Riz, and Barry M. Popkin. 2002. Trends in energy intake in U.S. between 1977 and 1996: similar shifts seen across age groups. *Obesity Research* 10 (5):370–8.

Nielsen, Samara Joy, and Barry M. Popkin 2004. Changes in beverage intake between 1977 and 2001. *American Journal of Preventive Medicine* 27 (3):205–10.

Popkin, Barry M., Pamela S. Haines, and Anna Maria Siega-Riz. 1999. Dietary patterns and trends in the United States: The UNC-CH Approach. *Appetite* 32:8–14.
My UNC team has approached the development of linked, nationally representative files of individual dietary intake in a unique way. This is a layout of the methods and approach for the scientist.

Siega-Riz, Anna Maria, Barry M. Popkin, and Terry A. Carson. 2000. Differences in food patterns at breakfast by sociodemographic characteristics among a nationally representative sample of adults in the United States. *Preventive Medicine* 30 (5):415–24.

USDA Economic Research Service. 2005. U.S. per capita food consumption: Beverages (individual): USDA.

———. 2006. Food Consumption (Per Capita) Data System: USDA.

On beverages, obesity, and health:

Bray, George A., Samara J. Nielsen, and Barry M. Popkin. 2002. High-fructose corn sweeteners and the epidemic of obesity. *American Journal of Clinical Nutrition* 79:537–43.

This article speculated on the possible effects of high-fructose corn syrup. Activists picked it up and took our speculation as truths and created dozens of websites about the effects of HFCS on obesity. The science that has appeared subsequently has told us that HFCS does not affect satiety and obesity but might have some other adverse health effects, discussed in the book.

Debette, Stephanie, et al. 2008. Tea consumption is inversely associated with carotid plaques in women. *Arteriosclerosis, Thrombosis, and Vascular Biology* 28 (2):353–9.

Negoianu, Dan, and Stanley Goldfarb. 2008. Just add water. *Journal of the American Society of Nephrology* 19:1041–43.

This is one of those modest editorials that get picked up and made into a huge deal by the media. In blogs, articles, radio programs, and newspaper articles, the authors were quoted as using a rather incomplete understanding of the health effects of water, based on a rather superficial understanding of the research on this topic. A large number of studies are either published or in press that show how misleading these scholars were in their knowledge of the health role of water.

Popkin, Barry M., Lawrence E. Armstrong, George M. Bray, Benjamin Caballero, Balz Frei, and Walter C. Willett. 2006. A new proposed guidance system for beverage consumption in the United States. *American Journal of Clinical Nutrition* 83 (3):529–42.

Rivera, Juan A., O. Muñoz-Hernández, M. Rosas-Peralta, C. A. Aguilar-Salinas, Barry M. Popkin, and Walter C. Willett. 2008. Consumo de bebidas para una vida saludable: recomendaciones para la población (Beverage consumption for a healthy life: recommendations for the Mexican population). *Salud Pública de México* 50 (2):173–95.

The Mexican beverage guidelines represent the first official government report on the subject. The Mexican government has used these to take major action to reduce consumption of caloric beverages.

Sanigorski, Andrea M., A. Colin Bell, and Boyd A. Swinburn. 2007. Association of key foods and beverages with obesity in Australian schoolchildren. *Public Health Nutrition* 10 (2):152–7.

Stookey, Jodi D., Florence Constant, Christopher Gardner, and Barry M. Popkin. 2007. Replacing sweetened caloric beverages with drinking water is associated with lower energy intake. *Obesity* 15 (12):2013–3032.

Stookey has a number of papers in press that essentially show that increased water intake appears to not only have effects in reducing intake of caloric beverages but also added metabolic effects such that consuming water, even over other diet beverages, may be linked with improvements in weight control, diabetes, and other cardiovascular and metabolic outcomes. There are a number of randomized controlled studies under way in the United States and Mexico that will be important for this topic.

3. ON MOVEMENT

Historical studies on time use in lower-income countries:

Evenson, R. E., Barry M. Popkin, and E. King-Quizon. 1980. Nutrition, work and demographic behavior in rural Philippines households. In *Rural Households Studies in Asia,* ed. H. P. Binswanger, R. E. Evenson, C. A. Florencio, and B. N. F. White. Singapore: Singapore University Press.

Gordon, K. D. 1987. Evolutionary perspectives on human diet. In *Nutritional Anthropology*, ed. F. E. Johnston. New York: Liss.

Herrin, Alejandro N. 1979. Rural electrification and fertility change in the Southern Philippines. *Population and Development Review* 5:61–86.

Sources and References

The classic case study on the effect of electrification on time-use patterns.

McCrone, John. 2000. Fired Up: Theory on when prehistoric man first used fire. *New Scientist* 166:30.

Thompson, John, Ina T. Porras, James K. Tumwine, Mark R. Mujwahuzi, Munguti Katui-Katua, Nick Johnstone, and Libby Wood. 2002. *Drawers of Water: 30 Years of Change in Domestic Water Use and Environmental Health—Summary*: United Nations Environmental Program: Earthprint.com.

White, Gilbert, David Bradley, and Anne White. 1972. *Drawers of Water: Domestic Water Use in East Africa*. Chicago: The University of Chicago Press.

The most in-depth classic study on domestic water use and the amount of time and effort needed to obtain water in low-income countries.

On trends in time use and energy expenditure in the past several decades:

Alenezi, Mohammad, and Michael L. Walden. 2004. A New Look at Husbands' and Wives' Time Allocation. *The Journal of Consumer Affairs* 38:81–107.

Brownson, Ross C., Tegan K. Boehmer, and Douglas A. Luke. 2005. Declining rates of physical activity in the United States: What are the contributors? *Annual Review of Public Health* 26 (1):421–43.

This is the most complete review I have seen of trends in physical activity in the United States. It is for scientists.

Gordon-Larsen, Penny, Robert G. McMurray, and Barry M. Popkin. 2000. Determinants of adolescent physical activity and inactivity patterns. *Pediatrics* 105 (6):E83.

Marshall, Joe, and Ken Hardman. 2000. The State and Status of Physical Education in Schools in International Context. *European Physical Education Review* 6 (3):203–29.

Monda, K. L., F. Zhai, and B. M. Popkin. 2008. Longitudinal relationships between occupational and domestic physical activity patterns and body weight in China. *European Journal of Clinical Nutrition* doi:10.1038/sj.ejcn.1602849.

Popkin, Barry M. 1999. Urbanization, lifestyle changes and the nutrition transition. *World Development* 27:1905–16.

———. 2006. Global nutrition dynamics: the world is shifting rapidly toward a diet linked with noncommunicable diseases. *American Journal of Clinical Nutrition* 84 (2):289–98.

On the effects of changing physical activity on obesity and health:

Lanningham-Foster, Lorraine, Lana J. Nysse, and James A. Levine. 2003. Labor saved, calories lost: the energetic impact of domestic laborsaving devices. *Obesity Research* 11 (10):1178–81.

Levine, James A., Lorraine M. Lanningham-Foster, Shelly K. McCrady, Alisa C. Krizan, Leslie R. Olson, Paul H. Kane, Michael D. Jensen, and Matthew M. Clark. 2005. Interindividual variation in posture allocation: possible role in human obesity. *Science* 307 (5709):584–86.

Levine and his group are the ones who have done the most to highlight the importance of small changes in activity patterns on energy expenditures and energy balance.

Nelson, Melissa C., Penny Gordon-Larsen, Yan Song, and Barry M. Popkin. 2006. Built and social environments: Associations with adolescent overweight and activity. *American Journal of Preventive Medicine* 31 (2):109–17.

Patterson, Paul D., Charity G. Moore, Janice C. Probst, and Judith Ann Shinogle. 2004. Obesity and physical inactivity in rural America. *Journal of Rural Health* 20 (2):151–9.

4. THE WORLD IS FLAT—AND FAT

On the historical dimensions of globalization:

The Chanda book is written for the nonspecialist.

Anon. 2005. Ancient noodle rewrites history. *New Scientist.*

Chanda, Nayan. 2007. *Bound Together: How Traders, Preachers, Adventurers, and Warriors Shaped Globalization.* New Haven: Yale University Press.

A well-written book about the global history of trade and globalization. The reader should think of this as a combination of a historical view and more in-depth argument about globalization than Thomas Friedman's book *The World Is Flat*.

Trager, James. 1997. *The Food Chronology: A Food Lover's Compendium of Events and Anecdotes, from Prehistory to the Present*. New York: Owl Books.

Broad studies of globalization and its effects:
The Friedman book is written for the nonspecialist.

Brownell, Kelly D., and Katherine Battle Horgen. 2003. *Food Fight: The Inside Story of the Food Industry, America's Obesity Crisis, and What We Can Do About It*. New York: McGraw-Hill.

An obesity scholar's review of some of the major arguments of the global food industry and their effects on health and obesity. This is very accessible to the general public.

Bu, W. 2002. *Effect of Mass Media on Children*. Beijing, China: Xinhua Publishing House.

Friedman, Thomas L. 2005. *The World Is Flat*. New York: Farrar, Straus and Giroux.

This is the most famous book on the topic. A best seller that laid out some of the major recent shifts in communications, distribution, and transportation in very broad terms.

Popkin, Barry M. 2006. Technology, transport, globalization and the nutrition transition. *Food Policy* 31:554–69.

Weber, I. G. 2000. Challenges facing China's television advertising industry in the age of spiritual civilization: An industry analysis. *International Journal of Advertising*: 19 (2):259–81.

Sources and References

Food industry case studies:
Both books are written for the nonspecialist.

Fishman, Charles. 2006. *The Wal-Mart Effect: How the World's Most Powerful Company Really Works—and How It's Transforming the American Economy.* New York: Penguin.

Watson, James L., ed. 1997. *Golden Arches East: McDonald's in East Asia.*, ed. Stanford, CA: Stanford University Press.

On the modern food distribution sector and its impact:
Tom Reardon has completed dozens of studies and created a focus on understanding the dynamics of the rise of supermarkets across the developing world. His work is very descriptive and there is as of yet little research on the impact of this sector on dietary practices in the depth needed to fully understand how eating behavior and ultimately obesity will be affected by the expansion of these types of food shopping outlets globally.

Asfaw, Abay. 2007. Supermarket expansion and the dietary practices of households: some empirical evidence from Guatemala. Washington, DC: International Food Policy Research Institute.

Balsevich, Fernando, Julio A. Berdegué, Luis Flores, Denise Mainville, and Thomas Reardon. 2003. Supermarkets and produce quality and safety standards in Latin America. *American Journal of Agricultural Economics* 85 (5):1147–54.

Hu, D. 2004. The rapid rise of supermarkets in China: challenges and opportunities for agricultural development and strategy. *Electronic Journal of Agricultural Developmental Economics.*

Hu, D., T. Reardon, S. Rozelle, P. Timmer, and H. Wang. 2004. The emergence of supermarkets with Chinese characteristics: challenges and opportunities for China's agricultural development. *Development Policy Review* 22:557–86.

Reardon, Thomas, and J. A. Berdegué. 2002. The rapid rise of supermarkets in Latin America: challenges and opportunities for development. *Development Policy Review* 20:371–88.

Sources and References

Reardon, Thomas, P. Timmer, J. Berdegué. 2004. The rapid rise of supermarkets in developing countries: induced organizational, institutional, and technological change in agrifood systems. *Electronic Journal of Agricultural and Development Economics* 1 (2):168–83.

Reardon, Thomas, C. P. Timmer, C. B. Barrett, and J. A. Berdegué. 2003. The rise of supermarkets in Africa, Asia, and Latin America. *American Journal of Agricultural Economics* 85:1140–46.

Tillotson, James E. 2008. Supermarkets in the 21st century: part 3. *Nutrition Today* 43 (1):29–35.

Wax, Emily. 2007. In India, a retail revolution takes hold: small vendors feel squeeze of chains. *Washington Post*, May 23, D.1.

Wilkinson, John. 2004. The food processing industry, globalization and developing countries. *Electronic Journal of Agricultural and Development Economics* 1 (2):184–201.

———. 2004. Globalization, food processing and developing countries: driving forces and the impact on small farms and firms. *Electronic Journal of Agricultural Developmental Economics* 1 (2):154–67.

On the restaurant and fast-food sectors and obesity:

There are a large number of descriptive studies of the ways consumption in restaurants is linked cross-sectionally and longitudinally with dietary intake. Most of this is for scholars.

The entire literature lacks clear causal work which addresses questions such as: Are those who eat in fast-food restaurants impacted adversely by fast-food restaurants or are they just different and seek out this type of food all the time? In other words, are fast-food eaters different from people who eat at restaurants, and is it these differences, preferences, etc. that create the added obesity? Or is it the food at the restaurants, their portion sizing, etc.?

Adair, Linda S., and Barry M. Popkin. 2005. Are child eating patterns being transformed globally? *Obesity Research* 13 (7):1281–99.

Duffey, Kiyah J., Penny Gordon-Larsen, David R. Jacobs Jr., O. Dale Williams, and Barry M. Popkin. 2007. Differential associations of fast-food and restaurant-food consumption with 3-year change in body mass index: the Coronary Artery Risk Development in Young Adults Study. *American Journal of Clinical Nutrition* 85 (1):201–8.

French, Simone A., Mary Story, Dianne Neumark-Sztainer, J. A. Fulkerson, and P. Hannan. 2001. Fast-food restaurant use among adolescents: associations with nutrient intake, food choices, and behavioral and psychosocial variables. *International Journal of Obesity* 25 (12):1823–33.

Jeffery, Robert W., and Simone A. French. 1998. Epidemic obesity in the United States: are fast foods and television viewing contributing? *American Journal of Public Health* 88 (2):277–80.

Lobstein, T., L. Baur, and Ricardo Uauy. 2004. Obesity in children and young people: a crisis in public health. *Obesity Reviews* 5 (Suppl 1):4–97.

Prentice, Andrew M., and S. A. Jebb. 2003. Fast foods, energy density and obesity: a possible mechanistic link. *Obesity Reviews* 4 (4):187–94.

Case studies of globalization, and of edible oils:

Drewnowski, Adam, and Barry M. Popkin. 1997. The nutrition transition: new trends in the global diet. *Nutrition Reviews* 55 (2):31–43.

Kim, Sowoon, Soojae Moon, and Barry M. Popkin. 2000. The nutrition transition in South Korea. *American Journal of Clinical Nutrition* 71 (1):44–53.

Lee, Min-June, Barry M. Popkin, and Soowon Kim. 2002. The unique aspects of the nutrition transition in South Korea: the retention of healthful elements in their traditional diet. *Public Health Nutrition* 5 (1A):197–203.

Ng, Shu Wen, Fengying Zhai, and Barry M. Popkin. 2008. Impacts of China's edible oil pricing policy on nutrition. *Social Science & Medicine* 66 (2):414–26.

Popkin, Barry M., and Adam Drewnowski. 1997. Dietary fats and the nutrition transition: new trends in the global diet. *Nutrition Reviews* 55:31–43.

Popkin, Barry M. 2004. The nutrition transition: an overview of world patterns of change. *Nutrition Reviews* 62 (7 Pt 2):S140–3.

Rastogi, Tanuja, K. Srinath Reddy, Mario Vaz, Donna Spiegelman, D. Prabhakaran, Walter C. Willett, Meir J. Stampfer, and Alberto Ascherio.

2004. Diet and risk of ischemic heart disease in India. *American Journal of Clinical Nutrition* 79 (4):582–92.

U.S. Department of Agriculture. 1996. 1996 U.S. fats and oils statistics. In *U.S. Department of Agriculture Statistical Bulletin No. 376*. Washington, DC: ERS.

Wallingford, John C., R. Yuhas, S. Du, F. Zhai, and B. M. Popkin. 2004. Fatty acids in Chinese edible oils: evidence for unexpected impact in changing diet. *Food and Nutrition Bulletin* 25:330–36.

5. THE BIG PROBLEMS OF A FAT WORLD

On U.S. and global obesity and chronic disease patterns:

There are hundreds of papers describing the global increases in obesity in the past several decades. The studies by Fogel and Bua et al. are unique in providing insights into the long-term increases in obesity over the past century or longer. Many of the earlier studies on global obesity in the developing countries were by me, but I haven't included them here. Instead, I've focused on more recent papers. The Monteiro and Popkin papers are very important for showing that across the globe the poor are more likely to be overweight than the rich. In other words, obesity is a global problem of the poor and not the rich.

Barquera, Simón, V. Tovar-Guzmán, I. Campos-Nonato, C. González-Villalpando, and Juan Rivera-Dommarco. 2003. Geography of diabetes mellitus mortality in Mexico: an epidemiologic transition analysis. *Archives of Medical Research* 34 (5):407–14.

Boyle, James P., Amanda A. Honeycutt, K. M. Venkat Narayan, Thomas J. Hoerger, Linda S. Geiss, Hong Chen, and Theodore J. Thompson. 2001. Projection of diabetes burden through 2050: impact of changing demography and disease prevalence in the U.S. *Diabetes Care* 24 (11):1936–40.

Bua, Jenny, Lina W. Olsen, and Thorkild I. A. Sorensen. 2007. Secular trends in childhood obesity in Denmark during fifty years in relation to economic growth. *Obesity* 15 (4):977–85.

Davis, Sharon K., Marilyn A. Winkleby, and John W. Farquhar. 1995. Increasing disparity in knowledge of cardiovascular disease risk factors and risk-reduction strategies by socioeconomic status: implications for policymakers. *American Journal of Preventive Medicine* 11 (5):318–23.

Doak, Colleen M., Linda S. Adair, Margaret Bentley, Carlos Monteiro, and Barry M. Popkin. 2005. The dual burden household and the nutrition transition paradox. *International Journal of Obesity* 29 (1):129–36.

Fogel, Robert W. 1994. Economic growth, population theory, and physiology: The bearing of long-term processes on the making of economic policy. *American Economic Review* 84:369.

———. 2004. *The Escape from Hunger and Premature Death, 1700–2100: Europe, America, and the Third World.* New York: Cambridge University Press.

Hale, Daniel E. 2004. Type 2 diabetes and diabetes risk factors in children and adolescents. *Clinical Cornerstone* 6 (2):17–30.

Harris, Kathleen M., Penny Gordon-Larsen, Ki Chantala, and J. Richard Udry. 2006. Longitudinal trends in race/ethnic disparities in leading health indicators from adolescence to young adulthood. *Archives of Pediatrics Adolescent Medicine* 160 (1):74–81.

Hedley, Allison A., Cynthia L. Ogden, Clifford L. Johnson, Margaret D. Carroll, Lester R. Curtin, and Katherine M. Flegal. 2004. Prevalence of overweight and obesity among U.S. children, adolescents, and adults, 1999–2002. *Journal of the American Medical Association* 291 (23):2847–50.

Kaufman, Jay S., Ramón A. Durazo-Arvizu, D. L. McGee, and Richard S. Cooper. 1997. The differences in diabetes risk in blacks and whites. *Annals of Epidemiology* 7 (1):76–7.

Kearney, Patricia M., Megan Whelton, Kristi Reynolds, Paul Muntner, Paul K. Whelton, and Jiang He. 2005. Global burden of hypertension: analysis of worldwide data. *Lancet* 365 (9455):217–23.

Kearney, Patricia M., Megan Whelton, Kristi Reynolds, Paul K. Whelton, and Jiang He. 2004. Worldwide prevalence of hypertension: a systematic review. *Journal of Hypertension* 22 (1):11–9.

Lipscombe, Lorraine L., and Janet E. Hux. 2007. Trends in diabetes prevalence, incidence, and mortality in Ontario, Canada 1995–2005: a population-based study. *Lancet* 369 (9563):750–6.

Lipton, Rebecca B., Melinda Drum, Deborah Burnet, Barry Rich, Andrew

Sources and References

Cooper, Elizabeth Baumann, and William Hagopian. 2005. Obesity at the onset of diabetes in an ethnically diverse population of children: what does it mean for epidemiologists and clinicians? *Pediatrics* 115 (5):e553–60.

Lobstein, T., L. Baur, and Ricardo Uauy. 2004. Obesity in children and young people: a crisis in public health. *Obesity Reviews* 5 (Suppl 1):4–97.

Mendez, Michelle A., Carlos A. Monteiro, and Barry M. Popkin. 2005. Overweight exceeds underweight among women in most developing countries. *American Journal of Clinical Nutrition* 81 (3):714–21.

Monteiro, Carlos A., Wolney L. Conde, Bing Lu, and Barry M. Popkin. 2004. Obesity and inequities in health in the developing world. *International Journal of Obesity Related Metabolic Disorders* 28 (9):1181–6.

Monteiro, Carlos A., Maria Helena D'A. Benicio, Wolney L. Conde, and Barry M. Popkin. 2000. Shifting obesity trends in Brazil. *European Journal of Clinical Nutrition* 54 (4):342–6.

Monteiro, Carlos A., E. C. Moura, Wolney L. Conde, and Barry M. Popkin. 2004. Socioeconomic status and obesity in adult populations of developing countries: a review. *Bulletin of the World Health Organization* 82 (12):940–6.

Moss, Mark H. 2003. Trends in childhood asthma: prevalence, health care utilization, and mortality. *Pediatrics* 112 (2):479.

Narayan, K. M. Venkat, James P. Boyle, Linda S. Geiss, Jinan B. Saaddine, and Theodore J. Thompson. 2006. Impact of recent increase in incidence on future diabetes burden: U.S., 2005-2050. *Diabetes Care* 29 (9):2114–6.

Narayan, K. M. Venkat, James P. Boyle, Theodore J. Thompson, Stephen W. Sorensen, and David F. Williamson. 2003. Lifetime risk for diabetes mellitus in the United States. *Journal of the American Medical Association* 290 (14):1884–90.

Neumark-Sztainer, Dianne, Jillian Croll, Mary Story, Peter J. Hannan, Simone A. French, and Cheryl Perry. 2002. Ethnic/racial differences in weight-related concerns and behaviors among adolescent girls and boys: findings from Project EAT. *Journal of Psychosomatic Research* 53 (5):963–74.

NIH. 2007. Calculate your body mass index (BMI) http://www.nhlbisupport .com/bmi/bmicalc.htm

Sources and References

Ogden, Cynthia L., Katherine M. Flegal, Margaret D. Carroll, and Clifford L. Johnson. 2002. Prevalence and trends in overweight among U.S. children and adolescents, 1999–2000. *Journal of the American Medical Association* 288 (14):1728–32.

Pinhas-Hamiel, Orit, and Philip Zeitler. 2007. Acute and chronic complications of type 2 diabetes mellitus in children and adolescents. *Lancet* 369 (9575):1823–31.

Pinhas-Hamiel, Orit, Lawrence M. Dolan, Stepehn R. Daniels, Debra Standiford, Philip R Khoury, and Philip Zeitler. 1996. Increased incidence of non-insulin-dependent diabetes mellitus among adolescents. *The Journal of Pediatrics* 128 (5):608–15.

Popkin, Barry M., Conde Wolney, Hou Ningqi, and Carlos Monteiro. 2006. Is there a lag globally in overweight trends for children as compared to adults? *Obesity* 14:1846–53.

Rivera, Juan, Simón Barquera, Teresa González-Cossio, Gustavo Olaiz, and Jaime Sepúlveda. 2004. Nutrition transition in Mexico and other Latin American countries. *Nutrition Reviews* 62 (7):s1–s9.

Sobal, Jeffrey, and Albert J. Stunkard. 1989. Socioeconomic status and obesity: a review of the literature. *Psychological Bulletin* 105 (2):260–75.

Stamatakis, E., P. Primatesta, S. Chinn, R. Rona, and E. Falascheti. 2005. Overweight and obesity trends from 1974 to 2003 in English children: what is the role of socioeconomic factors? *Archives of Disease in Childhood* 90 (10):999–1004.

Wang, Youfa, and May A. Beydoun. 2007. The obesity epidemic in the United States gender, age, socioeconomic, racial/ethnic, and geographic characteristics: a systematic review and meta-regression analysis. *Epidemiologic Reviews* 29 (1):6–28.

Wang, Youfa, and Tim Lobstein. 2006. Worldwide trends in childhood overweight and obesity. *International Journal of Pediatric Obesity* 1 (1):11–25.

Sources and References

On the health and economic consequences of obesity:

The Finkelstein and Zuckerman book is written for the nonspecialist.

American Diabetes Association position statement. 2004. Nephropathy in Diabetes. *Diabetes Care* 27 (90001):79S–83.

Baker, Jennifer L., Lina W. Olsen, and Thorkild I. A. Sorensen. 2007. Childhood body-mass index and the risk of coronary heart disease in adulthood. *The New England Journal of Medicine* 357 (23):2329–37.

Bray, George A. 2007. The missing link—lose weight, live longer. *The New England Journal of Medicine* 357 (8):818–20.

Finkelstein, Eric A., and Laurie Zuckerman. 2008. *The Fattening of America: How the Economy Makes Us Fat, If It Matters, and What to Do About It*. New York: John Wiley & Sons. Finkelstein has focused his career to a large extent on doing analyses of the economic costs of obesity. This book is a readable version of much of this work and adds many other topics.

Ford, Earl S., Umed A. Ajani, Janet B. Croft, Julia A. Critchley, Darwin R. Labarthe, Thomas E. Kottke, Wayne H. Giles, and Simon Capewell. 2007. Explaining the decrease in U.S. deaths from coronary disease, 1980–2000. *The New England Journal of Medicine* 356 (23):2388–98.

Franco, Oscar H., Ewout W. Steyerberg, Frank B. Hu, Johan Mackenbach, and Wilma Nusselder. 2007. Associations of diabetes mellitus with total life expectancy and life expectancy with and without cardiovascular disease. *Archives of Internal Medicine* 167 (11):1145–1151.

Fritscher, Leandro G., Cláudio C. Mottin, Simone Canani, and José M. Chatkin. 2007. Obesity and obstructive sleep apnea-hypopnea syndrome: the impact of bariatric surgery. *Obesity Surgery* 17 (1):95–9.

Haines, Krista L., Lana G. Nelson, Rodrigo Gonzalez, Tracy Torrella, Taylor Martin, Ali Kandil, Robert Dragotti, William M. Anderson, Scott F. Gallagher, and Michel M. Murr. 2007. Objective evidence that bariatric surgery improves obesity-related obstructive sleep apnea. *Surgery* 141 (3):354–8.

Hillier, Teresa A., and Kathryn L. Pedula. 2003. Complications in young adults with early-onset type 2 diabetes: losing the relative protection of youth. *Diabetes Care* 26 (11):2999–3005.

Sources and References

Hillier, Teresa A., Kathryn L. Pedula, Mark M. Schmidt, Judith A. Mullen, Marie-Aline Charles, and David J. Pettitt. 2007. Childhood obesity and metabolic imprinting: The ongoing effects of maternal hyperglycemia. *Diabetes Care* 30 (9):2287–92.

Kasasbeh, Aiman, Ehab Kasasbeh, and Guha Krishnaswamy. 2007. Potential mechanisms connecting asthma, esophageal reflux, and obesity/sleep apnea complex—a hypothetical review. *Sleep Medicine Reviews* 11 (1):47–58.

Kawahara, Reiko, Teiko Amemiya, Masayo Yoshino, Munehiro Miyamae, Kazuo Sasamoto, and Yasue Omori. 1994. Dropout of young non-insulin-dependent diabetics from diabetic care. *Diabetes Research and Clinical Practice* 24 (3):181–5.

Levay, Adam J., and John F. Kveton. 2008. Relationship between obesity, obstructive sleep apnea, and spontaneous cerebrospinal fluid otorrhea. *Laryngoscope* 118 (2):275–8.

Ludwig, David S. 2007. Childhood obesity—the shape of things to come. *The New England Journal of Medicine* 357 (23):2325–27.

Olshansky, S. Jay, Douglas J. Passaro, Ronald C. Hershow, Jennifer Layden, Bruce A. Carnes, Jacob Brody, Leonard Hayflick, Robert N. Butler, David B. Allison, and David S. Ludwig. 2005. A potential decline in life expectancy in the United States in the 21st century. *The New England Journal of Medicine* 352 (11):1138–45.

Popkin, Barry M., Susan Horton, and Soowon Kim. 2001. The nutrition transition and prevention of diet-related chronic diseases in Asia and the Pacific. *Food and Nutrition Bulletin* 22 (4(Suppl)):1–58.

Popkin, Barry M., Susan Horton, Soowon Kim, A. Mahal, and Jin Shuigao. 2001. Trends in diet, nutritional status, and diet-related noncommunicable diseases in China and India: the economic costs of the nutrition transition. *Nutrition Reviews* 59 (12):379–90.

Popkin, Barry M., Soowon Kim, E. R. Rusev, Shufa Du, and Claire Zizza. 2006. Measuring the full economic costs of diet, physical activity and obesity-related chronic diseases. *Obesity Reviews* 7 (3):271–93.

Singer, Natasha. 2007. Skin Deep: Feel pudgy? There's a shot for that. *New York Times*, September 20.

Sources and References

On the causes of obesity:

Barquera, Simón, Karen E. Peterson, Aviva Must, Beatrice L. Rogers, M. Flores, R. Houser, E. Monterrubio, and Juan Rivera-Dommarco. 2007. Coexistence of maternal central adiposity and child stunting in Mexico. *International Journal of Obesity* 31, 601–607. doi:10.1038/sj.ijo.0803529.

Cohen, Steven L., Jeffrey L. Halaas, Jeffrey M. Friedman, Brian T. Chait, Larry Bennett, David Chang, Randy Hecht, and Frank Collins. 1996. Human leptin characterization. *Nature* 382 (6592):589.

Frayling, Timothy M., Nicholas J. Timpson, Michael N. Weedon, Eleftheria Zeggini, Rachel M. Freathy, Cecilia M. Lindgren, John R. B. Perry, Katherine S. Elliott, Hana Lango, Nigel W. Rayner, Beverley Shields, Lorna W. Harries, Jeffrey C. Barrett, Sian Ellard, Christopher J. Groves, Bridget Knight, Ann-Marie Patch, Andrew R. Ness, Shah Ebrahim, Debbie A. Lawlor, Susan M. Ring, Yoav Ben-Shlomo, Marjo-Riitta Jarvelin, Ulla Sovio, Amanda J. Bennett, David Melzer, Luigi Ferrucci, Ruth J. F. Loos, Inês Barroso, Nicholas J. Wareham, Fredrik Karpe, Katharine R. Owen, Lon R. Cardon, Mark Walker, Graham A. Hitman, Colin N. A. Palmer, Alex S. F. Doney, Andrew D. Morris, George Davey Smith, The Wellcome Trust Case Control Consortium, Andrew T. Hattersley, and Mark I. McCarthy. 2007. A common variant in the FTO gene is associated with body mass index and predisposes to childhood and adult obesity. *Science* 316 (5826):889–94.

Friedman, Jeffrey M. 1997. Leptin, leptin receptors and the control of body weight. *European Journal of Medical Research* 2 (1):7–13.

Friedman, Jeffrey M., and Jeffrey L. Halaas. 1998. Leptin and the regulation of body weight in mammals. *Nature* 395 (6704):763–70.

Gordon-Larsen, Penny, Melissa C. Nelson, Phil Page, and Barry M. Popkin. 2006. Inequality in the built environment underlies key health disparities in physical activity and obesity. *Pediatrics* 117 (2):417–24.

Heisler, Michele, Jessica D. Faul, Rodney A. Hayward, Kenneth M. Langa, Caroline Blaum, and David Weir. 2007. Mechanisms for racial and ethnic disparities in glycemic control in middle-aged and older Americans in the health and retirement study. *Archives of Internal Medicine* 167 (17):1853–60.

Sources and References

Knowler, William C., Elizabeth Barrett-Connor, Sarah E. Fowler, Richard F.
Hamman, John M. Lachin, Elizabeth A. Walker, and David M. Nathan.
2002. Reduction in the incidence of type 2 diabetes with lifestyle
intervention or metformin. *The New England Journal of Medicine* 346
(6):393–403.

Kolata, Gina. 2007. *Rethinking Thin: The New Science of Weight Loss—And the
Myths and Realities of Dieting.* New York: Farrar, Straus & Giroux.

Stocker, Claire J., Ed Wargent, Jacqueline O'Dowd, Claire Cornick, John
R. Speakman, Jonathan R. S. Arch, and Michael A. Cawthorne. 2007.
Prevention of diet-induced obesity and impaired glucose tolerance in rats
following administration of leptin to their mothers. *American Journal of
Physiology, Regulatory, Integrative, and Comparative Physiology* 292 (5):
R1810–18.

Taubes, Gary. 2007. *Good Calories, Bad Calories.* New York: Knopf.
A well-documented book written by a journalist. It proposes an approach
toward causes of diet that defy current rules of thermodynamics and biology.

Taveras, Elise, Sheryl L. Rifas-Shiman, Emily Oken, Erica P. Gunderson, and
Matthew W. Gillman. 2008. Short sleep duration in infancy and risk of
childhood overweight. *Archives of Pediatrics and Adolescent Medicine*
162 (4):305–11.

Tuomilehto, Jaakko, Jaana Lindstrom, Johan G. Eriksson, Timo T. Valle, Helena
Hamalainen, Pirjo Ilanne-Parikka, Sirkka Keinanen-Kiukaanniemi, Mauri
Laakso, Anne Louheranta, Merja Rastas, Virpi Salminen, Sirkka Aunola,
Zygimantas Cepaitis, Vladislav Moltchanov, Martti Hakumaki, Marjo
Mannelin, Vesa Martikkala, Jouko Sundvall, Matti Uusitupa, and the
Finnish Diabetes Prevention Study Group. 2001. Prevention of type 2
diabetes mellitus by changes in lifestyle among subjects with impaired
glucose tolerance. *The New England Journal of Medicine* 344 (18):1343–50.

Wolk, Robert R., and Virend K. Somers. 2003. Cardiovascular consequences of
obstructive sleep apnea. *Clinics in Chest Medicine* 24 (2):195–205.

Wolk, Robert, Abu S. M. Shamsuzzaman, and Virend K. Somers. 2003. Obesity,
sleep apnea, and hypertension. *Hypertension* 42 (6):1067–74.

World Cancer Research Fund–American Institute for Cancer Research. 2007.

Food, Nutrition, Physical Activity and the Prevention of Cancer: A Global Perspective. Washington, D.C. World Cancer Research Fund in association with the American Institute for Cancer Research.

On obesity (bariatric) surgery:

This is the most effective viable treatment we have today for handling the problems of the very obese. When undertaken by skilled and experienced surgeons, this is very cost effective and often changes the lives of those who undertook the surgery. The largest and most complete study on this topic is from Sweden under Lars Sjostrom.

Finkelstein, Eric A., and Derek S. Brown. 2005. A cost-benefit simulation model of coverage for bariatric surgery among full-time employees. *American Journal of Managed Care* 11 (10):641–6.

Finkelstein, Eric A., Derek S. Brown, Yoav Avidor, and Annie H. Takeuchi. 2005. The role of price, sociodemographic factors, and health in the demand for bariatric surgery. *American Journal of Managed Care* 11 (10):630–7.

Karlsson, J., C. Taft, A. Ryden, L. Sjostrom, and M. Sullivan. 2007. Ten-year trends in health-related quality of life after surgical and conventional treatment for severe obesity: the SOS intervention study. *International Journal of Obesity* 31 (8):1248–61.

Kuhlmann, Hans W., Rainer A. Falcone, and Anna M. Wolf. 2000. Cost-effective bariatric surgery in Germany today. *Obesity Surgery* 10 (6):549–52.

Powers, Kinga A., Scott T. Rehrig, and Daniel B. Jones. 2007. Financial impact of obesity and bariatric surgery. *Medical Clinics of North America* 91 (3):321–38, ix.

Sjostrom, Lars, Anna-Karin Lindroos, Markku Peltonen, Jarl Torgerson, Claude Bouchard, Bjorn Carlsson, Sven Dahlgren, Bo Larsson, Kristina Narbro, Carl David Sjostrom, Marianne Sullivan, Hans Wedel, and the Swedish Obese Subjects Study Scientific Group. 2004. Lifestyle, diabetes, and cardiovascular risk factors 10 years after bariatric surgery. *The New England Journal of Medicine* 351 (26):2683–93.

Sources and References

Broad-based articles on the problems associated with obesity:

Zimmet, Paul Z. 1992. Kelly West Lecture 1991. Challenges in diabetes
    epidemiology—from West to the rest. *Diabetes Care* 15 (2):232–52.

Zimmet, Paul Z., Daniel J. McCarty, and Maximilian P. de Courten. 1997.
    The global epidemiology of non-insulin-dependent diabetes mellitus and the
    metabolic syndrome. *Journal of Diabetes and its Complications* 11 (2):60–8.

6. NOTHING TO SEE HERE: THE FOOD INDUSTRY'S ROLE IN CAUSING AND SOLVING THE PROBLEM

Essentially, to date there is no serious book written on how to get the global food industry to address global obesity issues. A friend and very wise former food and beverage industry executive, Hank Cardello, is publishing a book in 2009 with Doug Garr on this very topic. Otherwise, the references I use here are all related to specific points. These include an important book on global food companies by Tim Lang and his collaborator and the articles by Lesser et al. and Vartanian et al. that document the ways the beverage and sugar industries' support of research has distorted the findings of those who undertook this research.

The Pendergrast book is written for the nonspecialist.

American Dietetic Association. 2004. Use of nutritive and nonnutritive
    sweeteners. *Journal of the American Dietetic Association* 104 (2):255–75.

Boseley, Sarah. 2003. Sugar industry threatens to scupper WHO. *The Guardian*
    April 21.

Cardello, Hank, and Doug Garr. In Press (2009). *Stuffed: An Insider's Look at
    Who's (Really) Making America Fat.* New York: HarperCollins.
    This is the first book by a food industry executive trying to come to grips with
    the obesity epidemic and how the food industry can change to address this.

Committee on Food Marketing and the Diets of Children and Youth. 2005.
    Food Marketing to Children and Youth: Threat or Opportunity? Washington,
    DC: The National Academies Press.

Committee on Nutrition Standards for Foods in Schools, Virginia A. Stallings
    and Ann L. Yaktine, eds. 2007. *Nutrition Standards for Foods in Schools:*

Leading the Way Toward Healthier Youth. Washington, DC: The National Academies Press.

Food and Nutrition Board. 2004. *Preventing Childhood Obesity: Health in the Balance*. Washington, DC: The National Academies Press.

Lang, Tim, Geof Rayner, and Elizabeth Kaelin. 2006. The Food Industry, Diet, Physical Health: a Review of Reported Commitments and Practice of 25 of the World's Food Companies. London: Centre for Food Policy, City University.

Lang, Tim, and Michael Heasman. 2004. Food wars: the global battle for mouths, minds, and markets. *Earthscan*, August, 392.

Lesser, Lenard I., Cara B. Ebbeling, Merrill Goozner, David Wypij, and David S. Ludwig. 2007. Relationship between funding source and conclusion among nutrition-related scientific articles. *PLoS Medicine* 4 (1):e5.

Nestle, M. 2007. *Food Politics: How the Food Industry Influences Nutrition and Health*. Berkeley: University of California Press. 2nd ed.

This classic study, an exceptionally thorough discussion of the food industry, is very useful for anyone who wants to understand in depth the myriad ways in which that industry may affect people's behavior.

Nielsen, Samara J., Anna Maria Siega-Riz, and Barry M. Popkin. 2002. Trends in energy intake in U.S. between 1977 and 1996: similar shifts seen across age groups. *Obesity Research* 10 (5):370–8.

———. 2002. Trends in food locations and sources among adolescents and young adults. *Preventive Medicine* 35 (2):107–13.

Pendergrast, Mark 2000. *For God, Country & Coca-Cola: The Definitive History of the Great American Soft Drink and the Company That Makes It*. New York: Basic Books.

Sanigorski, Andrea M., A. Colin Bell, and Boyd A. Swinburn. 2007. Association of key foods and beverages with obesity in Australian schoolchildren. *Public Health Nutrition* 10 (2):152–7.

Vartanian, Lenny R., Marlene B. Schwartz, and Kelly D. Brownell. 2007. Effects of soft drink consumption on nutrition and health: a systematic review and meta-analysis. *American Journal of Public Health* 97 (4):667–75.

Sources and References

7. WHAT CAN WE DO?

What can individuals and communities do?

Two of the most popular and potentially important activities we can do in our local communities are promoting walking to school for kids and healthy environments in our schools and neighborhoods. While researchers have shown that a large number of other factors are important, such as reducing crime, creating playgrounds, and creating supervised after-school play, much of the focus has been on either healthy eating in schools or physical activity during and after school. It is my hope this energy will be expanded to promoting healthy vending and snacking in schools and in entire communities. Crime is a huge deterrent to activity among children. In the United States, we are in a very primitive stage in terms of parental and community actions. France is one of the leaders in this activity, as discussed in the book.

Ahlport, Kathryn N., Laura Linnan, Amber Vaughn, Kelly R. Evenson, and Dianne S. Ward. 2008. Barriers and facilitators of walking and bicycling to school: formative results from the NMT Study. *Health Education and Behavior* 35 (2):221–44.

Brody, Gene H., Shannon Dorsey, Rex Forehand, and Lisa Armistead. 2002. Unique and protective contributions of parenting and classroom processes to the adjustment of African American children living in single-parent families. *Child Development* 73 (1):274–86.

Center for Science in the Public Interest. 2007. Sweet Deals: School Fundraising can be profitable and healthy. Washington, DC: CSPI.

Jilcott, S. B., Barbara A. Laraia, Kelly R. Evenson, Lisa M. Lowenstein, and Alice S. Ammerman. 2007. A guide for developing intervention tools addressing environmental factors to improve diet and physical activity. *Health Promotion Practice* 8 (2):192–204.

Saksvig, Brit I., Diane J. Catellier, Karin Pfeiffer, Kathryn H. Schmitz, Terry Conway, Scott Going, Dianne Ward, Patty Strikmiller, and Margarita S. Treuth. 2007. Travel by walking before and after school and physical activity among adolescent girls. *Archives of Pediatrics & Adolescent Medicine* 161 (2):153–58.

Ward, Dianne S., Laura Linnan, Amber Vaughn, Brian Neelon, Sarah L. Martin, and Janet E. Fulton. 2007. Characteristics associated with U.S. Walk to School programs. *International Journal of Behavioral Nutrition and Physical Activity* 4:67.

What can states and regional entities do?

Cummins, Steven, and Sally Macintyre. 2002. Food deserts—evidence and assumption in health policy making. *British Medical Journal* 325:436–38.

Rodriguez, Daniel A., Asad J. Khattak, and Kelly R. Evenson. 2006. Can new urbanism encourage physical activity? Comparing a new urbanist neighborhood with conventional suburbs. *Journal of the American Planning Association* 72:43–54.

Can we help the health sector help us?

Ammerman, Alice, A. Caggiula, P. Elmer, P. Kris-Etherton, T. Keyserling, C. Lewis, R. Luepker, T. Pearson, B. Shucker, B. Shannon, R. Simpson, and J. Watson. 1994. Putting medical practice guidelines into practice: the cholesterol model. *American Journal of Preventive Medicine* 10:209–16.

Ammerman, Alice, Robert DeVellis, T. Carey, Thomas Keyserling, D. Strogatz, Pamela Haines, R. Simpson, and D. Siscovick. 1993. Physician-based diet counseling for cholesterol reduction: Current practices, determinants, and strategies for improvement. *Preventive Medicine* 22:96–109.

Ammerman, Alice S., Thomas C. Keyserling, Jan R. Atwood, James D. Hosking, Hany Zayed, and Cristina Krasny. 2003. A randomized controlled trial of a public health nurse directed treatment program for rural patients with high blood cholesterol. *Preventive Medicine* 36 (3):340–51.

Davison-Krahnstoeverk, Kirsten, Tanja M. Cutting, and Leann L. Birch. 2003. Parents' activity-related parenting practices predict girls' physical activity. *Medicine & Science in Sports & Exercise* 35 (9):1589–95.

Elliott, Stuart. 2008. McDonald's ending promotion on jackets of children's report cards. *New York Times*, January 18.

Epstein, Leonard H., Elizabeth A. Handley, Kelly K. Dearing, David D. Cho, James N. Roemmich, Rocco A. Paluch, Samina Raja, Youngju Pak, and Bonnie Spring. 2006. Purchases of food in youth: influence of price and income. *Psychological Science* 17 (1):82–89.

Sources and References

Epstein, Leonard H., Rocco A. Paluch, Brian E. Saelens, Michelle M. Ernst, and Denise E. Wilfley. 2001. Changes in eating disorder symptoms with pediatric obesity treatment. *Journal of Pediatrics* 139 (1):58–65.

Epstein, Leonard H., Rocco A. Paluch, Constance C. Gordy, and Joan Dorn. 2000. Decreasing sedentary behaviors in treating pediatric obesity. *Archives of Pediatrics Adolescent Medicine* 154 (3):220–6.

Epstein, Leonard H., and James N. Roemmich. 2001. Reducing sedentary behavior: role in modifying physical activity. *Exercise and Sport Sciences Reviews* 29 (3):103–8.

Epstein, Leonard H., James N. Roemmich, Rocco A. Paluch, and Hollie A. Raynor. 2005. Influence of changes in sedentary behavior on energy and macronutrient intake in youth. *Americal Journal of Clinical Nutrition* 81 (2):361–66.

Evenson, Kelly R., Robert W. Motl, Amanda S. Birnbaum, and Dianne S. Ward. 2007. Measurement of perceived school climate for active travel in children. *American Journal of Health Behavior* 31 (1):86–97.

Evenson, Kelly R., Sara L. Huston, Bradley J. McMillen, Philip Bors, and Dianne S. Ward. 2003. Statewide prevalence and correlates of walking and bicycling to school. *Archives of Pediatrics & Adolescent Medicine* 157 (9):887–92.

Keyserling, Thomas C., Alice S. Ammerman, Jan R. Atwood, James D. Hosking, Cristina Krasny, Hany Zayed, and Betty H. Worthy. 1999. A cholesterol intervention program for public health nurses in the rural southeast: description of the intervention, study design, and baseline results. *Public Health Nursing* 16 (3):156–67.

Nagourney, Eric. 2007. Growing pains: Many parents fail to see obesity in children. *New York Times*, December 18.

Nemet, Dan, Sivan Barkan, Yoram Epstein, Orit Friedland, Galit Kowen, and Alon Eliakim. 2005. Short- and long-term beneficial effects of a combined dietary-behavioral-physical activity intervention for the treatment of childhood obesity. *Pediatrics* 115 (4):e443–49.

Parker-Pope, Tara. 2006. Passing the ball: hip campaign that got kids to be active looks for its next move. *The Wall Street Journal*, September 6.

Perrin, Eliana M., Kori B. Flower, and Alice S. Ammerman. 2005. Pediatricians' own weight: self-perception, misclassification, and ease of counseling. *Obesity Research* 13 (2):326–32.

Savoye, Mary, Melissa Shaw, James Dziura, William V. Tamborlane, Paulina Rose, Cindy Guandalini, Rachel Goldberg-Gell, Tania S. Burgert, Anna M. G. Cali, Ram Weiss, and Sonia Caprio. 2007. Effects of a weight management program on body composition and metabolic parameters in overweight children: a randomized controlled trial. *Journal of the American Medical Association* 297 (24):2697–704.

Stewart-Brown, S., J. Patterson, C. Mockford, J. Barlow, I. Klimes, and C. Pyper. 2004. Impact of a general practice based group parenting programme: quantitative and qualitative results from a controlled trial at twelve months. *Archives of Disease in Childhood* 89 (6):519–25.

On healthy diets:

Aravanis, Christ, Adrian Corcondilas, A. S. Dontas, Demetrios Lekos, and Ancel Keys. 1970. Coronary heart disease in seven countries. IX. The Greek islands of Crete and Corfu. *Circulation* 41 (4 Suppl):I88–100.

Dansinger, Michael L., Joi Augustin Gleason, John L. Griffith, Harry P. Selker, and Ernst J. Schaefer. 2005. Comparison of the Atkins, Ornish, Weight Watchers, and Zone diets for weight loss and heart disease risk reduction: a randomized trial. *Journal of the American Medical Association* 293 (1):43–53.

Fidanza, F., V. Puddu, A. B. Imbimbo, A. Menotti, and A. Keys. 1970. Coronary heart disease in seven countries. VII. Five-year experience in rural Italy. *Circulation* 41 (4 Suppl):163–75.

Gardner, Christopher D., Alexandre Kiazand, Sofiya Alhassan, Soowon Kim, Randall S. Stafford, Raymond R. Balise, Helena C. Kraemer, and Abby C. King. 2007. Comparison of the Atkins, Zone, Ornish, and LEARN diets for change in weight and related risk factors among overweight premenopausal women: the A TO Z Weight Loss Study: a randomized trial. *Journal of the American Medical Association* 297 (9):969–77.

Keys, Ancel. 1962. Diet and coronary heart disease throughout the world. *Cardiologia Pratica* 13:225–44.

Sources and References

———. 1980. W. O. Atwater memorial lecture: overweight, obesity, coronary heart disease and mortality. *Nutrition Reviews* 38 (9):297–307.

Roberts, Susan B., Lisa Tracy, and Melvin B. Heyman. 1999. *Feeding Your Child For Lifelong Health: Birth Through Age Six*. New York: Bantam Books.

On economic actions and related analyses:

Burke, Mary A., and Frank Heiland. 2007. Social dynamics of obesity. *Economic Inquiry* 45:571–91.

Caplovitz, David. 1967. *The Poor Pay More*. New York: Free Press.

Chaloupka, F. J., K. M. Cummings, C. P. Morley, and J. K. Horan. 2002. Tax, price and cigarette smoking: evidence from the tobacco documents and implications for tobacco company marketing strategies. *Tobacco Control* 11 Suppl 1:I62–72.

Chung, Chanjin, and Samuel L. Myers. 1999. Do the poor pay more for food? An analysis of grocery store availability and food price disparities. *Journal of Consumer Affairs* 33 (2):276–296.

Cox, Thomas L., and Michael K Wohlgenant. 1986. Prices and quality effects in cross-sectional demand analysis. *American Journal of Agricultural Economics* 68 (4):908–19.

Finkelstein, Eric A., and Laurie Zuckerman. 2008. *The Fattening of America: How the Economy Makes Us Fat, If It Matters, and What to Do About It*. New York: John Wiley & Sons.

Finkelstein, Eric A., Derek S. Brown, and Barry M. Popkin. 2007. Lifetime medical costs associated with obesity and smoking. Draft manuscript.

Finkelstein, Eric A., Derek S. Brown, Justin G. Trogdon, Joel E. Segel, and Rami H. Ben-Joseph. 2007. Age-specific impact of obesity on prevalence and costs of diabetes and dyslipidemia. *Value Health* 10 Suppl 1:S45–51.

Grossman, M., and F. J. Chaloupka. 1997. Cigarette taxes. The straw to break the camel's back. *Public Health Reports* 112 (4):290–7.

Guo, Xuguang, Barry M. Popkin, Thomas A. Mroz, and Fengying Zhai. 1999. Food price policy can favorably alter macronutrient intake in China. *Journal of Nutrition* 129 (5):994–1001.

Sources and References

Timmer, C. Peter, W. P. Falcon, and S. R. Pearson. 1984. *Food Policy Analysis*. Baltimore: The Johns Hopkins University Press for the World Bank.

On national and global actions:

Gilmore, I. 2007. What lessons can be learned from alcohol control for combating the growing prevalence of obesity? *Obesity Reviews* 8 (s1):157–60.

Powell, Lisa M., Glen Szczypka, Frank J. Chaloupka, and Carol L. Braunschweig. 2007. Nutritional content of television food advertisements seen by children and adolescents in the United States. *Pediatrics* 120 (3):576–83.

Puska, Pekka. 2002. WHO's strategy on nutrition and noncommunicable diseases prevention. *IARC Scientific Publications* 156:519–21.

WHO/FAO. 2003. Expert Consultation on Diet, Nutrition and the Prevention of Chronic Diseases Report of the Joint WHO/FAO Expert Consultation, WHO Technical Report Series, No. 916 (TRS 916). Geneva: World Health Organization.

On lessons from other public health actions:

Doll, Richard, and A. Bradford Hill. 1950. Smoking and carcinoma of the lung. Preliminary report. *British Medical Journal* 2 (4682):739–48.

Lantz, Paula M., Peter D. Jacobson, Kenneth E. Warner, Jeffrey Wasserman, Harold A. Pollack, Julie Berson, and Alexis Ahlstrom. 2000. Investing in youth tobacco control: a review of smoking prevention and control strategies. *Tobacco Control* 9 (1):47–63.

Liang, Lan, Frank Chaloupka, Mark Nichter, and Richard Clayton. 2003. Prices, policies and youth smoking, May 2001. *Addiction* 98 Suppl 1:105–22.

Mercer, Shawna L., Lawrence W. Green, Abby C. Rosenthal, Corinne G. Husten, Laura Kettel Khan, and William H. Dietz. 2005. Drawing, possible lessons for obesity prevention and control from the tobacco control experience. In *Obesity Prevention in the 21st Century: Public Health Approaches to Tackle the Obesity Pandemic*, ed. D. Crawford and R. Jeffery. New York: Oxford University Press.

Report of the Advisory Committee to the Surgeon General of the Public Health

Sources and References

Service. 1964. Smoking and Health. In *Surgeon General of the Public Health Service*. Washington, DC: U.S. Department of Health and Human Services Public Health Service.

U.S. Department of Health and Human Services. 1982. The health consequences of smoking: cancer. A report of the surgeon general (DHHS Publication No (PHS) 82-50179), ed. United States Government Printing Office. Rockville, MD: Public Health Service, Office on Smoking and Health.

Warner, Kenneth E. 2005. Tobacco Policy in the United States: Lessons for the Obesity Epidemic. In *Policy Challenges in Modern Health Care*, ed. D. Mechanic, L. B. Rogut, D. C. Colby, and J. R. Knickman. New Brunswick, NJ: Rutgers University Press.

Wakefield, Melanie A., Frank J. Chaloupka, Nancy J. Kaufman, C. Tracy Orleans, Dianne C. Barker, and Erin E. Ruel. 2000. Effect of restrictions on smoking at home, at school, and in public places on teenage smoking: cross sectional study. *British Medical Journal* 321 (7257):333–7.

On the costs of inaction:

Colditz, Graham A. 1999. Economic costs of obesity and inactivity. *Medicine & Science in Sports & Exercise* 31 (11 Suppl):S663–7.

Katzmarzyk, Peter T., and Ian Janssen. 2004. The economic costs associated with physical inactivity and obesity in Canada: an update. *Canadian Journal of Applied Physiology* 29 (1):90–115.

Popkin, Barry M., Susan Horton, and Soowon Kim. 2001. The nutrition transition and prevention of diet-related chronic diseases in Asia and the Pacific. *Food and Nutrition Bulletin* 22 (4(Suppl)):1–58.

Popkin, Barry M., Susan Horton, Soowon Kim, A. Mahal, and Jin Shuigao. 2001. Trends in diet, nutritional status, and diet-related noncommunicable diseases in China and India: the economic costs of the nutrition transition. *Nutrition Reviews* 59 (12):379–90.

Thompson, David, John Edelsberg, Karen L. Kinsey, and Gerry Oster. 1998. Estimated economic costs of obesity to U.S. business. *American Journal of Health Promotion* 13 (2):120–7.

Sources and References

On the promotion of organic and natural and local production and consumption:

Probably one of the more active global sets of changes is the broad-based push toward eating and producing local. Termed the "locavore" movement by many, this in many ways originated with the "slow food" concepts of Carlo Petrini as a broad-based movement. In the United States, Alice Waters of Chez Panisse was one of the first to promote the eat-and-buy-local-and-fresh concept. Michael Pollan is the popular writer who has done the most to build on this and create wide knowledge and understanding of this issue. Local farmers' markets are not new; however, what is new are the pushes toward growing and selling locally and toward organic produce. Linked to this area many farm-to-market and farm-to-school initiatives are attempting to promote these topics in the local institutions.

The Petrini and Pollan books are written for the nonspecialist.

Petrini, Carlo. 2007. *Slow Food Nation: A Blueprint for Changing the Way We Eat*. New York: Rizzoli Ex Libris.

Pollan, Michael. 2006. *The Omnivore's Dilemma: A Natural History of Four Meals*. New York: Penguin Press.

———. 2008. *In Defense of Food: An Eater's Manifesto*. New York: Penguin Press.

Other articles used in this chapter:

Cummings, Steven R., David Bates, and Dennis M. Black. 2002. Clinical use of bone densitometry: scientific review. *Journal of the American Medical Association* 288 (15):1889–97.

Mozaffarian, Dariush, Martijn B. Katan, Alberto Ascherio, Meir J. Stampfer, and Walter C. Willett. 2006. Trans-fatty acids and cardiovascular disease. *The New England Journal of Medicine* 354 (15):1601–13.

Popkin, Barry M., Conde Wolney, Hou Ningqi, and Monteiro Carlos. 2006. Is there a lag globally in overweight trends for children as compared to adults? *Obesity* 14:1846–53.

INDEX

Index

Index

Index

Index

Index

child obesity and, 94
in developing countries, 94–95
educational programming in India, 14
typical patterns, 7–8, 10, 66–67
T.G.I. Friday's, 140
Third World Action Group, 132
Thompson, Tommy, 135
time- and laborsaving technologies
in household, 67, 69, 72–75
in workplace, 77–79
Together, Let's Prevent Obesity in Children
(EPODE), 158
trans fats, 155, 156
Trowell, Hugh, 29
Two Angry Moms (Kalfa and Rubin), 153
type 2 diabetes. *See* diabetes

UHT-treated milk (ultra-high temperature),
48, 89
Unilever, 138
Unsafe at Any Speed (Nader), 161
U.S. Department of Health and Human
Services, 135
U.S. Farm Bill, 131
U.S. Sugar Association, 134–35

vegetable oils
in diet of developing world, 86, 90–91
taxation of, 164

Veggie Mobile, 159–60
VERB campaign, 169

Wallerstein, David, 36
Wal-Mart, 11
Wansink, Brian, 40
water consumption, 43–46, 55–56
weekend eating, 35, 50
weight problems. *See* child obesity; obesity
Weil, Andrew, 51
Wendy's, 142–43
WHO (World Health Organization),
134–35, 172–73
Willett, Walter, 91, 132–33
William J. Clinton Foundation. *See* Clinton
Foundation
wine, 49–50, 81
Winner's Circle Healthy Dining Program,
160
workplace technology, 77–79
World Bank, 173
World Health Organization (WHO),
134–35, 172–73
World Is Flat, The (Friedman), 85
World Trade Organization (WTO), 98–99
Wyeth company, 138

Yach, Derek, 135
Yudkin, John, 31